The Death Cult

Technocratic failure at the end of the industrial age

Tim Watkins

© Tim Watkins 2023

ISBN: 9798375374901

All rights reserved. No part of this publication may be reproduced, stored in a retrieval system, or transmitted, in any form or by any means, electronic, mechanical, photocopying, recording or otherwise, without the prior permission of the copyright owner.

Waye Forward Ltd

www.wayeforward.com

Contents

Preface	1
The Bottleneck	11
The rise of the (fake) meritechnocracy	19
The end of the big idea	25
Technocracy for technocracy's sake	33
Designed to fail	63
Just make it stop	87
There's more to this picture	101
Imagined futures…	111
… and hard realities	125
The sum of the parts	151
Earthbound	167

About the author

Tim Watkins is the author of the *Consciousness of Sheep* website and the 2015 book of the same name, which addresses the unfolding environmental, energy and resource depletion, and economic crises that threaten the collapse of industrial civilisation; and possibly the extinction of the entire human race.

He graduated from University of Wales College Cardiff with a First Class economic science degree in 1990.

Between 1990 and 1997 he worked as a policy researcher with the Welsh Consumer Council where he wrote and published several key policy reports including: *Quality of Life and Quality of Service* – an investigation into the provision of residential care homes for older people - and *In Deep Water* – an investigation into the many problems that followed the North Wales (Towyn) floods of February 1990.

Between 1998 and 2010, Tim Watkins worked for the charity Depression Alliance Cymru, initially as a development worker, and between 2003 and 2010 as its Director. During that time he produced several mental health publications for the charity. Between 2001 and 2010 Tim Watkins was appointed to sit on several Welsh Government advisory bodies including the Health and Wellbeing Council for Wales, the Burrows-Greenwell Review of Mental Health Services in Wales and the Expert Panel on Depression.

Since 2010, Tim Watkins has authored a range of books relating to the "three E's" - Energy, Environment and the Economy. He has also produced a range of mental health and well being self-help books and booklets, together with two books on charity.

To find out more, please visit:

www.consciousnessofsheep.co.uk

You can also follow Tim Watkins on social media:

www.facebook.com/cosheep

www.youtube.com/@consciousnessofsheep

Preface

The legacy of a certain failed Austrian painter who rose to prominence in Germany in the 1930s, hangs over us today like a thick fog. It blinds us to the forces which have almost completed the transition away from democracy to something far more dangerous. This is because so many of us lowered our guard because we expected the next version of despotism to arrive in fancy dress, complete with armbands and jackboots. But history never repeats in that way, particularly because rulers and ruled alike got burned – metaphorically and literally – last time around. And those at the top were not about to repeat the mistake.

In any case, the German example was an outlier – a peculiar confluence of the rampant antisemitism and cultural blind obedience which had prevailed for generations, together with the unique economic decline of post-First World War Germany. Other fascisms of the period – while unpalatable to any true democrat – tended to be less extreme, and more *nationally* rather than *racially* orientated. Where Hitler claimed to be the embodiment of the mythical Aryan race, less maniacal dictators claimed only to be the arbiters of the ongoing tensions between the various groups which made up their respective nations. Nor was this *corporatist* ideology anything new. As John Rawlston Saul argues[1]:

> "This early form of corporatism gradually emerged as the only serious alternative to democracy. It was increasingly proposed by the Catholic elites of Europe. They could accept the Industrial Revolution, so long as individualism was replaced by group membership... Many of these groups were apparently benign or even beneficial. Workers unions. Industrial owners associations. Professional associations. These corporations were not to function in conflict with each other. Through ongoing negotiations, they were to be non-threatening and non-confrontational bodies. Some

of this system was formalised by Bismarck in the new Germany of the 1870s. But the corporatist alternative's moment of glory, so to speak, came half a century later Under Mussolini and various other dictators, such as Portugal's Salazar."

Despite the protestations of establishment media outlets and what passes for a political "left" these days, who tell us that every rising politician from outside the cosy neoliberal consensus is "the new Hitler," there is not going to be a repeat of the rise of the dictators in the 1920s and 1930s. The ruling classes have learned that lesson all too well. Nevertheless, the drive to replace democracy with a corporatist alternative is as strong today as it was back then. As Saul points out:

> "The last thing today's neo-corporatists want is to be confused with these unpleasant dictators. Most of the intellectuals now involved in pushing this social formula are well-established university professors: political scientists, sociologists and economists, spread throughout the West. And yet, what they propose – bald violence of the earlier generation aside – is virtually identical to the earlier model. They propose a basic shifting of legitimacy in our society from the citizen to the group. They don't put it quite that way. They talk modestly about facilitating the relationship between competing interest groups. The effect, however, would be far more profound than that. In fact, I believe that we are already very close to having shifted the legitimacy inside Western society. Real power today rests with neo-corporatism, which is in fact old-fashioned corporatism."

That was quarter of a century ago. Bill Clinton had begun the process of cementing a new neoliberal consensus into place. But his partner in crime, Tony Blair, had only just been elected. At the time, various terms – neo-corporatist, neo-conservative and even neo-fascist – each subtly different, but each marking the same shift of legitimacy from the individual to the group, were being bandied around. In the hands of Clinton's Democrats and Blair's Labour, corporatism donned the façade of liberal democracy but with none of its substance in what became known as *neo-liberalism*. A better term would be *fake* liberalism. Fake, that is, in the sense of counterfeit – like the counterfeit Gucci handbags and Chanel perfume proffered by the illegal street vendors on London's Oxford Street... requiring an expert eye to spot the tell-tale signs of forgery.

Although eroded to a considerable extent, the trappings of liberal democracy – political parties, free elections, freedom of thought and action, the right to peaceful protest, etc. – *appear* to be in place. But they have either been limited, qualified, curtailed or by-passed. In the age of social media, the public square is controlled by corporate power. Corporate censorship has caused most of us to develop the binary mode of thinking described by the subjects of the Soviet Union, in which one keeps one's private opinions to oneself, while publicly parroting the approved party line... obviously there is no such thing as a woman. Clearly a vaccine need neither prevent disease, stop transmission, nor even be less safe than the disease itself. And windmills and electric vehicles will definitely cool the global temperature.

Power, meanwhile, rests with a new corporate elite whose spurious claim to specialist knowledge and expertise provides justification for their elevated status. Managers – who used to be the hired help, paid only to maximise shareholder profit – now hide behind an amorphous "stakeholder capitalism" which obliges them to be answerable to all, and thus accountable to nobody. Elected politicians meanwhile genuflect at the altar of new *globalist* bodies to which they have sold their souls along with the power once held by national electorates. And those global bodies – special corporate courts, international banks, customs unions and privileged think tanks – in turn, are well on the way to dismantling what remains of national democratic structures... borders, what borders?

The trick – which is where the fakery comes in – has been to *appear* to over-privilege the individual. In Thatcher's formulation, "there is no such thing as society..." Not just in a "free market" which has clearly been captured by corporate power to an extent which would have horrified classical liberals like Adam Smith. But neoliberalism also atomises society into powerless individuals whose only means of exercising agency is as a member of one or other group. This is a travesty of democratic liberalism, in which markets are free *from* monopoly and corporate capture, and in which *active* and *disinterested* individuals operate as a part of a free citizenry. That is, true liberal democracy operates in the *public* interest, not in the interest of special groups, each with varying degrees of power. As a measure of this, Saul points to the one part of the economy which has continued to grow:

> "A simple test of our situation would involve examining the health of the public good. For example, there has never been so much money – actual money – disposable cash – in circulation as there is today. I am measuring this both in absolute terms and on a per capita basis. Look at the growth of the banking industry and the even more explosive growth of money markets. There has never been so much disposable money, yet there is no money for the public good. In a democracy this would not be the case, because the society would be centred, by general agreement, on disinterest. In a corporatist system there is never any money for the public good because the society is reduced to the sum of the interests. It is therefore limited to measurable self-interest."

This is, of course, a crisis in itself. Because while neoliberals make the claim that democracy is the consequence of free markets, technology and industrialisation, the reverse is, in fact, the case. And this has serious ramifications for us today, as we face a growing list of potentially existential economic, energetic and environmental crises. One of the most obvious features of corporatism – both the 1930s version and today's – is its lack of creativity. Free – and particularly disruptive and innovative – thought is anathema to the corporate interest, and is therefore stifled and censored. So that, just at the point where we need creative solutions, we are served a lukewarm dish of groupthink so old it has evolved new species of mould on its surface.

Consider the non-solutions to climate change. Just as I am writing these words, for example, the representatives of western neoliberal corporatism have flown into the Swiss resort of Davos on more than a thousand private jets and have booked up all of the tables at the resort's five-star steak restaurants – along, allegedly, with the services of some of Europe's most expensive prostitutes[2] – for the entire week of the World Economic Forum's annual conference. A conference where they will tell we mere peasants that we can no longer eat meat or fly to our annual holidays. As I wrote six months ago[3], as Europe's energy crisis began to seriously impact the economy:

> "The giveaway was the dissonance between their words and their deeds. It was as if the rich folks who live in the swanky penthouse apartments had come running down to the lower floors screaming that the building was on fire and that everyone had to evacuate. But then, when all of the ordinary folks were left outside in the cold rainy night, dressed only in their pyjamas, the rich folks went back up to their penthouses and carried on as if nothing had happened. That was the so-called 'climate emergency,' the claim that 'we' – by which they meant

only the little people – had to act now – which always seemed to amount to more corporate welfare for them and more eco-austerity for everyone else – to prevent disaster by reaching 'net zero' by the end of the decade."

Climate change is real enough – although occurring on a far more gradual timescale than the WEF technocrats would have us believe – but the proposed "solutions" are entirely fake. To the untrained eye, the WEF technocracy's fourth industrial revolution/great reset/green new deal – which ignores almost all of the crises engulfing us – looks plausible enough. After all, we have been drip fed a diet of fake information about so-called renewable *electricity*-generating technologies by a similarly invested establishment media. It is only when we take the time to listen to energy experts – particularly physicists who understand the physical limits and engineers who have to find ways of putting policy into practice – that we discover that the proposed "net zero" goals are unworkable without rapidly de-industrialising and de-populating the western states; and very likely much of the rest of the world too.

This latter possibility has inevitably given rise to grand conspiracy theories. Some "they," hiding in the shadows – for whom the WEF technocracy are merely the paid administrators – has – for reasons unspecified – decided that they must engineer the rapid premature deaths of billions of people. Although it is hard to understand how this would benefit anyone. Not least because the wealth and power of those at the top ultimately rests on the mass consumption and mass indebtedness of the billions at the bottom who they are – according to the online conspiratorium – determined to kill off.

This is not to suggest that conspiracies don't occur, or that the conspiring among the rich and powerful is more likely to succeed than conspiracies lower down the pecking order. It is simply that social hierarchies tend to operate to thwart rather than assist conspiracy. The old masonic image of the all-seeing eye at the top of the pyramid – famously reproduced on American paper currency – was more akin to the little old man behind the curtain in *The Wizard of Oz* – a tool to frighten the masses – than a true representation of power. In reality, the hierarchy – like the human brain – acts to suppress and censor information at every level. Only a tiny fraction of the information that is available at the bottom ever makes it to the top. And the fraction that does, is that which was deemed acceptable to be passed upward at each level. As a senior civil servant once told me, "only send the minister those problems for which we have solutions."

The problem seems far more to do with the unintended consequences of the neoliberal "solutions" to the crises of the 1970s. the immediate aim – crushing wages in order to curb rampant inflation – appeared successful. Although the collapse in wages was far more to do with the oil shock-induced recessions brought about by the OPEC oil embargo and later the Iranian revolution and the Iran-Iraq war than with the mythological expertise of Saint Paul Volcker. I throw Volcker in here, because he is the archetypal neoliberal technocrat. Laying claim to some esoteric econometric knowledge and expertise, Volcker and his followers promoted the fake narrative that through manipulation of interest rates it was they – not the global recession – which defeated inflation in the early 1980s. Crucially, it was on the back of such claims that the technocrats began pursuing their claim that they alone knew how best to run the world, and that they should be allowed to operate from a position *above and beyond* the organs of democratic oversight which, they claimed, had been colonised by ignorant and often prejudiced plebians whose constant disputes stood in the way of progress.

What began with the central bankers and university economics departments gradually spread to every area of human activity. And gradually a technocracy has usurped the democratic order which had propelled the western states to greatness in the first place. True technocracy – rule by experts – could base its legitimacy on the claim that its aggregate knowledge and understanding of the workings of our increasingly complex society allows it to stand head and shoulders above the rest of us. But I will argue that today we have a *fake* technocracy. One whose response to a series of very real threats to civilisation has been to ignore problems entirely or to retreat into the realms of impossible fantasy utopias – dragging the rest of us along with them – in a way that makes the various threats ever more likely to bring about collapse.

It is for this reason that I refer to the technocracy, along with the various special interest groups it promotes as a Death Cult; either passively acquiescing in or actively creating the existential crises which are now washing over us. Around the world, there is growing awareness of the abject failure of our fake technocracy. In the developed Western states there have been growing political movements around some version of the desire to "Take Back Control." Although thus far, that political energy has been captured by charlatans, chancers and ne'er-do-wells who promise to make countries great again, but leave them in a worse state than they had been. Beyond the western states, much of the world's nations are also seeking some alternative. Although one suspects that swapping the Western empire for a new, China/Russia-led "BRICS" bloc, might be a case of out of the frying pan into the fire.

The question this book sets to answer, is how we came to arrive at this impasse. And, more importantly given the urgency of the crises before us, can we change things for the better? Or was Margaret Thatcher right all those years ago when she claimed that, "there is no alternative?"

Notes

1. Saul, J.R. 1997. *The Unconscious Civilisation*. Penguin Books.

2. Zilber, A. 18 January 2023. "Prostitutes charge Davos attendees $2,500 a night as sex work demand booms." *New York Post*. https://nypost.com/2023/01/18/prostitutes-charge-davos-attendees-2500-a-night

3. Watkins, T. 30 August 2022. "Net Zero is dead – so what now?" *Consciousness of Sheep*. https://consciousnessofsheep.co.uk/2022/08/30/net-zero-is-dead-so-what-now

The Bottleneck

In the summer of 1950, a group of the world's leading physicists, including Edward Teller, Herbert York, and Emil Konopinski, discussed and dismissed a spate of implausible UFO sightings reported in the news. It was during this conversation that Enrico Fermi interjected, "Yes, but where is everybody?" The logic behind the question was reasonably simple[1]:

> "There are somewhere between 200 and 400 billion stars in the Milky Way alone. There are perhaps 70 sextillion (7×10^{22}) in the observable universe. With numbers this big, even if life is an extremely rare phenomenon, there would still be enough life-bearing planets for technologically advanced civilisations to emerge in large numbers. And since the universe has been around for a long time, a reasonable proportion of those civilisations could be expected to be far in advance of their own. Given the numbers, we would anticipate that our solar system should have already been visited by space aliens. But even if we were somehow by-passed, our own observations ought by now to have yielded evidence of alien communication, or the evidence of non-natural structures such as orbiting space stations."

Despite this – a couple of unidentified "wow signals" aside – there is currently no evidence of life anywhere else in the universe, and certainly nothing technologically equivalent or greater than our own civilisation. This is now known as "Fermi's Paradox" – the universe ought to be teeming with intelligent life, but all we detect is the void.

Why should this be? Two obvious answers present themselves. First, the religious texts are correct – Earth is the only place where life exists, and human civilisation is at the very apex of creation. This seems unlikely given the scale even of our own galaxy, still less the universe itself.

And so, the second possibility is that we've been looking in the wrong place and/or using the wrong technology. This seems equally implausible, since, even if an alien civilisation was using some unknown advanced means of communication, they would surely have used radio at some point in their technological development. And in the same way as planet Earth has been broadcasting a cacophony of radio signals since May 1897, we might reasonably expect that similar background noise would be observable elsewhere.

There is a third, unnerving explanation for the apparent absence of intelligent extra-terrestrials. This is the bottleneck hypothesis. This holds that while the conditions for life may be widespread, and those for intelligent life common enough to allow technological civilisations to emerge, the cost of technological development is so great that any civilisation which embarks on the process of industrialisation sows the seeds of its own destruction via a series of converging crises which become harder to resolve the more complex the civilisation becomes. Today these include:

Resource depletion

Energy shortages

Soil depletion

Biodiversity loss

Microplastic contamination

Chemical pollution

Nutrient run-off

Ocean acidification

Water shortages

Famine

Antibiotic resistance

War

Weapons of mass destruction

Governance failure

Financial crises

Infrastructure failure

Natural disasters

Migration waves

Cyber-attacks, AI consequences, etc.

Of course, many of these have plagued humanity for the entire of its existence. But the less complex a society is, the more resilient it tends to be. For example, *localised* famines were commonplace across seventeenth century Europe. But nowhere were they so widespread as to threaten society as a whole. But with eight billion humans depending upon a globally interconnected food supply chain, shortages – for example if artificial fertiliser became too expensive, or if war disrupted supply – might easily bring about another "Arab Spring" event in which countries and even regions descend into revolution and governments are overthrown.

It is also true though, that even modern, complex, and highly integrated economies are usually resilient enough that they can absorb the shock of any one of these potential crises. But the point of the bottleneck hypothesis is that the process of integration and growing complexity *causes* many of these crises to beset us at the same time. And there are only so many different shocks that an economy can absorb before things begin to break down. A financial crisis, for example, results in an investment failure which causes critical infrastructure to fail. This failure occurs just at the point where the combined pollution of three centuries of industrialisation is causing the environment to become more hostile. The need to take urgent remedial action though, causes commodity shortages as each country seeks to outbid the others to secure the energy and minerals it needs. Even if war – very likely involving nuclear, chemical and biological weapons – is avoided, the combined impact of the other shocks is likely to cause a breakdown of complex civilisation and a return to a pre-industrial way of life that would have been recognisable to people in Middle Ages Europe.

The answer to Fermi's Paradox is most likely that, even if intelligent life is common, most civilisations self-destruct long before they reach the point where they can communicate – still less travel – across the vast distances of space. And there is no reason to believe that humanity will be any different. Because, while we might flatter ourselves by pretending that we use intelligence and rationality to resolve the problems that face us, in reality, most of what we do is determined by a base psychology which favours short-term pleasure-seeking and pain-avoiding responses which usually exacerbate our problems in the longer-term. The Davos crowd, for example, may pontificate at length about the need to curb the pollution caused by air travel and large motor cars. And yet they are somehow unable to forego the use of private jets and chauffeur-driven limos to ferry them around.

Indeed, the excessive focus on carbon dioxide pollution – which is just *one subset* of one of the bottleneck crises we are hurtling toward – is itself a grand version of what psychologists call a "displacement activity." This is something that occurs to an individual when the crises facing them become so overwhelming that they lose all control. In an attempt to restore some illusory control, they may focus obsessively on something that they retain a degree of agency over even as their lives are falling apart – such as, for example, someone obsessively polishing their cutlery while facing imminent bankruptcy and eviction. In a similar way, pretending to address the carbon-reduction element of the man-made portion of climate change helps us pretend that more imminent and equally deadly monetary, supply chain, energy, commodity, and infrastructure crises are not happening.

For those of us who grew up in the shadow of the two world wars, we had always expected that "cometh the hour, cometh the man" – that faced with a real threat to civilisation, we would recognise and turn to true leaders who would, in turn, rally humanity to the heroic efforts needed to prevail... or at least to die trying. Instead, what passes for modern day leadership is better summed up by G. Michael Hopf[2]:

> "Hard times create strong men. Strong men create good times. Good times create weak men. And, weak men create hard times."

In the face of the bottleneck of converging crises, our leaders are indeed weak, corrupt and selfish. No longer do we talk seriously about grand projects for the benefit of humanity. And even the few, puny, responses – electric vehicles, corn ethanol, wind turbines, etc. – seem designed more to enrich their proponents than to offer a genuine solution to anything. All too often all that remains of public policy and public investment is graft and petty theft by a feeble leadership class which falsely believes itself to have been elevated above the fray.

Meanwhile – as an increasing number of us know from our own experience – hard times are upon us once again.

This book is less about the raft of bottleneck crises which are becoming ever harder to ignore – I have written about these at length elsewhere[3]. Rather, it is about the means by which weak men came to usurp democracy and to impose a form of fake technocratic rule which is wholly inadequate to addressing the crises facing us. It is also a wake-up call to those who not only see the gathering storm but have woken up to the fact that those we have allowed to rule over us are incapable of leading us to anything other than disaster and despair.

I begin by examining the way the optimism of the post-war years was gradually replaced by cynical and empty promises. I show how this process was accompanied by the rise of what I call the "fake meritechnocracy" – a class of credentialed experts who claimed, despite all evidence to the contrary, to have risen to their positions of power and privilege solely by their own merit. I go on to detail how this class, whose initial claim to legitimacy was that their expertise brought benefits to all, became self-perpetuating and self-interested – more often acting to the detriment of the rest of us.

The rise of the technocracy was a product of the corporatist, neoliberal consensus which emerged out of the crises of the 1970s and 1980s. The arrival of technocratic politicians – specialists in getting elected – like Bill Clinton and Tony Blair – paved the way for the devolution of power to self-professed experts who all too often failed to deliver for the wider population, but nevertheless enjoyed rates of remuneration the rest of us could only dream of. Many commentators imagined that there would be some kind of revolution to overthrow the technocrats. But while protest has been common and loud, it has been wholly ineffective. The occupy protests in the wake of the 2008 crash, for example, drew massive support and yet achieved nothing – only in Iceland were a couple of bankers jailed, while elsewhere the bankers were given pay rises to clean up the mess they had caused. The backlash against the EU central bankers during the currency crisis in 2011 attracted similar widespread support – most prominently in Greece, where there was a massive vote in favour of leaving the euro – but ultimately, nothing changed. The Arab Spring of that year could at least claim the new government in Tunisia and a temporary interregnum in Egypt. Since then, protest has reverted to single issues – just stop oil, black lives matter, etc. – which again, for all the noise end up changing nothing.

One reason for the failure of protest is that the technocracy has successfully created a thwarted bourgeoisie out of the expanded university system – the kids who took the wrong courses and/or went to the wrong universities, and who didn't get the promised ticket to riches. It is from this class – white, relatively affluent, middle class, entitled – that the modern fake left emerged, largely as supporters of the technocracy's agenda, rather than as a genuinely radical force for change. Indeed, as progress has objectively stalled, it has become impossible to envision a realistic alternative to the current arrangements. And so, the technocracy and its supporters have abandoned all grasp on reality and have instead imagined futures which simply do not comport with reality. Worse still, they have begun the process of dismantling our life support systems even before beginning to calculate the energy and resources which would be required to create one or other of the techno-utopian fantasy futures they claim to be building.

Economist John Maynard Keynes once lamented that markets can be irrational far longer than you can remain solvent. It is a phenomenon we have witnessed many times since. A financial system almost entirely divorced from the real world appears to be capable of existing and growing even as the real world that it is based upon slumps. But eventually, hard reality forces markets to collapse in order to better reflect the state of the real world. Something similar appears to be occurring with the current class structure. The technocracy – and the thwarted bourgeoisie beneath it – is, indeed, certifiably insane. Nevertheless, its pursuit of entirely self-destructive policy and reform can continue even as the real world on which its fantasies are built is flashing warning lights... in the contest between technocracy and Mother Nature, I know which I am betting on.

Notes

1. Watkins, T. 23 February 2017. "Fermi's Paradox is alive and well… and that is bad news for all of us." https://consciousnessofsheep.co.uk/2017/02/23/fermis-paradox-is-alive-and-well-and-that-is-bad-news-for-all-of-us/

2. Hopf, G.M. 2016. *Those Who Remain*.

3. See my publications list at the end of this book, and eight years of essays and articles on the website: www.consciousnessofsheep.co.uk

The rise of the (fake) Meritechnocracy

It is 64 years since Michael Young's satire, *The Rise of the Meritocracy* was published. It was, no doubt, a response to the aspirations around the post-war expansion of education. The school leaving age had been raised, and an expansion of grammar schools provided a route for working class kids to access higher education. This *social* mobility had been accompanied by *geographical* mobility too, as kids from the old industrial regions of the UK went off to study in the affluent university towns of the south of England, and then later stayed there when they found work.

Britain never was a meritocracy, of course. The very presence of a Royal Family with a direct lineage back to the Norman Conquest and beyond, let everyone know that hereditary privilege was alive and well. Indeed, for all of the benefits of a grammar school education for those working class kids who passed the eleven-plus exam, there is little evidence for the levels of social mobility often claimed – the *proportion* of working class kids going on to university remained the same. It is just that the post-war economy required more graduates across the board.

Meritocracy though, was a tacit aim of a Labour Party which had, de facto, abandoned any appetite for the socialist utopia. Rather than the pursuit of *equality*, the post-war Labour Party sought only *equality of opportunity*. In education, this was quickly thwarted by Labour's own *middle class* activists, who provided the strongest support for the abolition of the distinction between grammar and secondary schools. The abolition of the eleven-plus exam was a classic example of the way in which middle class self-interest is presented as a concern for social justice. The exam itself had no pass mark, but instead was based on the number of grammar school places available in any year. This meant, for example, that kids could pass the exam in one year with a lower mark than those who had "failed" in the previous year. More politically contentious though, was the reality that working class kids from the local council estate could earn a place at the grammar school, thereby pushing out the middle class kids from the leafy suburbs.

Once the system of comprehensive education had been implemented, the middle class parents could use class advantage to ensure that their kids fared better than the working class kids – paying for extra tuition, buying up-to-date books, and simply better understanding how the exam game was played. Suffice to say that Young's book was not an examination of something which existed, but rather a critique of the policy if it had ever been successfully implemented. And the broad point – which would have been visible to him in the late-1950s – was that given the opportunity, the salaried classes will *always* seek to pull the ladder up behind them.

This, of course, is precisely what the neoliberal governments of Bill Clinton and Tony Blair sought to do in the 1990s. Not that the USA or the UK *were* meritocracies, but rather they created a system which allowed those in the twenty percent or so of the population still prospering after the economic vandalism of the 1980s, to become a self-replicating "class for itself" – ensuring its own offspring maintained their privileged position while the offspring of other classes were excluded.

By the time Blair returned his iteration of the Labour Party to government in 1997, even the pretence of socialism had been purged. While leading Labour figures were engaged in a "prawn cocktail offensive" to win the support of the City of London bankers, Britain's working class were told that they were on their own. The best they could hope to get from a Labour government was "education, education,

education" – in effect, to take on swathes of student debt, often in exchange for a degree which was largely worthless. This was because Blair's version of higher education was a cargo cult[1] – it was based on the logically flawed assumption that if Britain created an army of degree-educated people, an equivalent number of high-paying degree-level jobs would surely follow. Wishful thinking indeed. Economies simply don't work this way. And so, the expansion of education resulted in massive qualification-inflation, as employers offering roles which would previously have been filled by people with a good GCSE grade could choose from a surplus of people with bachelor's degrees. Meanwhile, the genuinely academically talented were required to take on even more debt and spend more time obtaining MSc and PhD qualifications for employment roles which had previously been taken by BSc graduates with a first or a good 2:1.

The self-replicating part of the process was that almost all of the genuinely graduate-level roles still went to the graduates of the old, top-tier universities. Meanwhile, the majority of the working class kids went off to second and third tier colleges whose post-graduation employment record has been far more patchy. Indeed, in purely financial terms, those working class kids who stayed at home and learned trades like plumbing, carpentry and electrics, tend to earn more than those who went off to a third-tier university.

Not that it ended there. With the expansion of education, and a far larger pool of graduates to choose from, organisations in the cultural and political heights of the economy were able to introduce retrogressive unpaid internships as the first rung on the career ladder. In practice, this meant that only those graduates whose parents were affluent enough to pay their expenses for a year could get on the career ladder... or at least get a head start. The next rung on the ladder might be open for applications from non-interns, but only an imbecile would believe that a known, tried and tested intern would not fare better.

The counter-intuitive outcome of this, anything but meritocratic system, is that its beneficiaries simply *pretended* that it was. As Thomas Frank was to write of the Clinton Democrats – which Blair's Labour copied[2]:

> "Every time our liberal leaders deregulated banks and then turned around and told working-class people that their misfortunes were all attributable to their poor education, that the only answer for them was a lot of student loans and the right sort of college degree... every time they did this they made the disaster a little more inevitable...

> "In an article he [William Galston, a DLC insider and neoliberal guru] co-wrote in 1998, he told Democrats that 'the new economy favours a rising learning class over a declining working class.' To keep up with 'new realities,' he wrote, Democrats needed to understand that labour was in decline, that the New Deal generation was dying, and that the future belonged to a certain group of affluent, well-educated people. The rest is history. New Democrats did indeed defeat populism. High-minded Democratic centrists did indeed abandon their traditional identification with working people in favour of the 'learning class.' And Democrats started finding it 'difficult' to take action on matters of basic economic fairness."

What was beginning to emerge at this point – and what has grown to a truly species-endangering extent since – is not just a denial of reality, but a genuine hatred of *anything* which reminds the technocracy that, when all is said and done, their pretend "self-identifying" lives are as bound to the material realities of Planet Earth as are everyone else's. The very presence of ordinary working people – those whose work turned out to be "essential" when SARS-CoV-2 arrived in 2020 – doing such menial things as growing and harvesting food, driving trucks and delivery vans, working in water treatment plants, providing healthcare in hospital wards, and all of the other things which allow most of us to enjoy lives which don't require hours gathering dirt beneath our fingernails, is abhorrent to a class that wishes to believe that it is where it is solely by its own doing.

In the 2020s, it is no longer possible to talk about the Western states as democracies – from the Ancient Greek "dēmos" the people, and "kratia" power or rule – when those who enjoy the commanding heights of the culture, politics and economies are now positively hostile toward ordinary people. Rather, we have a system of rule that the Greeks called "tekhnekratia" – a technocracy in which power and influence rest upon – in our case an *imagined* – technological and intellectual excellence. This flaw in democracy was well known to the ancient Greeks. Socrates put the problem this way. Suppose you had to take a sea voyage which would involve sailing through dangerous currents and past jagged rocks. Would you choose to crew your ship with experienced mariners and navigators (tekhne) or would you choose a crew which was representative of the wider population (demos)? Only someone with a death wish would choose the latter. The former is the only sensible option, even though it is undemocratic. The issue this poses is whether it is possible for the captain to ensure that the crew act in the interest of the wider population... and if so, how?

One answer concerns "interests." It is – or at least *was* – the case that technocratic organisations didn't so much act against the interests of the people, than that they only pursued those interests which happened to correspond to their own and those of the wider ruling elite. This though, was much easier to do during the boom years after the Second World War than it has been during the slow-motion train wreck of the past half century. The harder economic times have become, the more technocratic self-interest becomes a stick with which to beat down the interests of ordinary people... "trust the science, pleb!"

Our technocracy is worse than mere rule based on the right qualifications and internships though. Today's technocrats are what has been disparagingly – but not erroneously – referred to as "trust fund kids." They are the *inheritors* of wealth and privilege. People who have never worked on the factory floor, nor have they ever had to meet a wage bill. And while we might hope that people with such a weak grasp on how the real world works might have developed a considerable degree of humility, the opposite is true. The technocracy has gone out of its way to pretend that its privilege was earned on merit. And this self-delusion rapidly gave way to graft. As the technocracy has emerged as what Marx called "a class *for itself*," so the graft, which had always existed to some degree, has grown – increasingly visibly – to epidemic proportions.

Notes

1. Watkins, T. 1 May 2019. "Getting social mobility wrong." *Consciousness of Sheep*.
https://consciousnessofsheep.co.uk/2019/05/01/getting-social-mobility-wrong/

2. Frank, T. 27 April 2017. "The Democrats' Davos ideology won't win back the Midwest." And 23 May 2018. "Forget Trump – populism is the cure, not the disease"*Guardian*.
https://www.theguardian.com/commentisfree/2017/apr/27/democratic-party-2018-races-midwest-populism-trump and
https://www.theguardian.com/books/2018/may/23/thomas-frank-trump-populism-books

The end of the big idea

On 16 July 1969, a Saturn V rocket launched three American astronauts into space. Four days later, two of the men, Neil Armstrong and Buzz Aldrin would enter the history books as the first and second humans to set foot on the moon. The third, and perhaps less famous astronaut, Michael Collins, remained in orbit around the moon, from where he took the iconic photograph of an Earthrise over the moon's horizon. With the exception of Collins himself, every human alive at the time was included in that image.

The Apollo 11 mission was without question a triumph of both science and engineering, even if critics have since pointed to its Cold War undertones and the dubious pasts of several former Nazi scientists who worked on the project. Nevertheless, it was something of a climax for an American age in which one apparently only had to dream up a goal and provide it with sufficient resources, to make it a reality.

And yet in the end, the Apollo programme went nowhere. Who today remembers the third and fourth men to set foot on the moon? Apollo 12 (14 to 24 November 1969) was barely news at the time. And Apollo 13 is only remembered for the near-catastrophic explosion of its oxygen tank and the touch and go eventual rescue of its crew. Eugene Andrew Cernan remains the last human to set foot on the moon, taking off from the lunar surface just before 6.00pm EST on 14 December 1972. By then though, the world had entered a darker age.

From its inception in May 1961 to its end in December 1972, the Apollo programme had drawn on the efforts of more than 400,000 people working in more than 20,000 industrial corporations and universities. The programme cost around $25 billion – more than $175 billion today. It no doubt returned valuable science and engineering, but both at the time and subsequently, the jury has been out as to whether it was worth it.

The moon itself turned out to be as barren as it appeared from Earth. There was no hint of life, or even of the precious mineral resources which might have made the trip worthwhile. In the years immediately after the Apollo programme, it could still be sold as a starting base for humanity's predestined journey to the stars. But that dream died pretty quickly too. Insofar as humans have gone into "space" since 1972, it is only the 408km or so to the International Space Station – a long way short of the 384,400km to the moon.

Commercial supersonic flight shared a similar timeline. France and the UK signed the treaty to share the development cost of the *Concorde* in November 1962, and the airliner made its maiden flight in March 1969. An early example of government projects to follow, the initial budget of £70 million proved wildly optimistic. By 1976, *Concorde* had cost British and French taxpayers around £2 billion – around £14 billion today. What it delivered in return was no more than a white elephant. Despite provisional orders for 66 *Concordes* from 18 airlines between 1963 and 1972, all but 12 – six each for the French and British state airlines – were cancelled when it became clear that commercial supersonic flight was too expensive to operate. Nevertheless, the British and French *Concordes* continued to traverse the Atlantic as a public-subsidised perk for wealthy business executives, movie stars and bankers, until the British and French governments pulled the plug in 2003.

Manned *deep* space flight and commercial supersonic flight point to a difference in the meaning of "can" and "can"[1] which will have considerable importance to the argument made in this book. It points to a very real distinction between what is *technically* and what is *economically* possible.

That is, we didn't unlearn how to send humans to the moon in 1972 any more than we unlearned how to propel humans between Europe and the USA faster than the speed of sound in 2003. Both are still technically achievable. Indeed, in the subsequent decades our technical abilities have likely increased. The reason we no longer do either is simply that the cost of doing them outweighs the benefits.

For those schooled in the religion of a finance-based economy, this quibbling over cost just sounds mean. "They can always find the money to fight wars," being a common objection (although this proposition is being heavily tested at the time of writing). If only we had the political will to reinstate *Concorde* or to return humans to the moon, then surely, we could make it happen. This suggestion though, serves only to demonstrate that *political will* is also subject to the material constraints which, despite the protestations of the econometric clerisy, set the hard boundaries of human activity.

Supersonic flight and moon landings, moreover, were self-contained programmes for turning big ideas into action. Sat alongside the two, both in time and massive government spending, is Lyndon Johnson's attempt to create a *Great Society*. Rather than a single project, the Great Society envisioned in Johnson's 1964 speech at Ohio University was an attempt to create a peacetime interventionism different to the US government's emergency responses to the Great Depression and the Second World War. It also stands as an early example of the fallacy that legislation and funding alone are sufficient to bring about the desired change.

The Great Society legislation covered what in the UK was known as the welfare state – the post-war attempt to slay Beveridge's "five giants" – want, disease, ignorance, squalor and idleness. In the USA, where apartheid had persisted through the 1950s, several packages of civil rights legislation were also enacted to formally end segregation and to bolster voting rights. Environmental and consumer legislation was also enacted. But the desired outcomes largely failed. Despite the America of the 1960s standing as the wealthiest economy the world had ever seen, poverty persisted even as average incomes rose. While general health improved, the health outcomes for the poorest remained far below average. Across the economy, indeed, despite the legislation and billions of dollars, it was the technocratic salaried class which benefitted the most from programmes which were ostensibly intended to raise the poorest up to the level of the salaried class. And, of course, when the economic tide turned in the early 1970s, it was that same salaried class which began to pull the ladder up behind them.

In the UK, Harold Wilson's attempt to unleash the "white heat of technology," suffered a similar fate. Unlike the USA, whose economy had boomed in the aftermath of the Second World War, a large part of the British economy consisted of legacy coal-powered Victorian industries like coal mining, ship building, railway working and steelmaking. This came with the geographical and political division between north and south, with the old industries in the north of the country failing even as new industries like aviation, petrochemicals and pharmaceuticals were growing in the midlands and the south. In the 1950s, the Tory government response was to encourage the de-population of the old industrial towns and cities of northern England in order to provide a workforce for the growing modern industries in the south. Wilson's pitch, in contrast, was that a partnership between state and industry – akin to that which was succeeding in West Germany and Japan – could replace the old northern industries with state-of-the-art new industries based around leading edge technologies. Prophetically, Wilson imagined automobile manufacturing plants which could produce cars without a human hand ever touching them – although it would be several decades later before fully automated assembly plants put in an appearance.

Despite the rhetoric – which returned the Labour Party to power for the first time in 13 years – political pressure and a rear-guard defence of the old order by organised labour put paid to Wilson's corporatist vision of a grand partnership between state, capital and labour in pursuit of economic growth and prosperity. *Concorde*, indeed, being just one example of the manner in which state ambitions and funding could be co-opted into corporate welfare and graft.

One of the ways in which the Tories succeeded in savaging Britain's Victorian railway network, was to blow up the bridges the moment a line was officially closed. This put the cost of reopening a line far higher than anyone was prepared to pay. Faced with trades unions which funded his party, Wilson was unable to do the same for state-controlled industries like coal mining, steel working and ship building, which cost far more to run than they could generate in sales. In large part, the nationalised industries became a means of curbing unemployment even as inflationary pressures began to mount on the UK economy. Unable to dispense with the technologically bankrupt old, Wilson lacked the political space to develop the technologically advanced new.

Both the Great Society in the USA and Wilson's attempt at technological renewal in the UK not only came to be seen as failures but have subsequently been used by opponents of state intervention to "prove" that governments always make a hash of anything they turn their hand to. Poverty, illiteracy, ill-health and homelessness continued unabated, seemingly untouched by the millions of dollars and pounds pumped into the well-meaning organisations which purported to have solutions to such things. And as failure became endemic, graft set in. Indeed, failure extended to far smaller state-led projects, with such things as new roads, railways and nuclear power stations inevitably running over-time and over-budget. All too often, state funding appeared to be more an attempt to funnel money to favoured lobbying organisations – including "sock-puppet" non-profits set up or funded by the state itself – rather than to solve the many social and economic woes increasingly besetting a post-peak western industrial civilisation.

The moon landings and *Concorde* had gone over budget too, of course. And no doubt there was graft. But unlike later state-led projects, these earlier programs were – to borrow some management speak – measurable and *time bound*. Hollywood fiction aside, we were able to measure the success of the Apollo program because men landed on the Moon in July 1969. We could judge *Concorde* to have succeeded when – albeit a little late – French and British airlines began flying passengers over the Atlantic at supersonic speeds. How, in contrast, would we know if the wars on poverty, drugs, crime and terror had succeeded? Indeed, might not the various lobby groups which benefit from such "wars" engage in mission creep in order to continue receiving state-funding? When was the last time you heard of a charity which announced that it was no longer needed because the problem it was established to deal with had been solved?

The end of the big idea favoured the political class too. A politician who promises to halve unemployment or double GDP growth by the end of their term in office would likely be deemed to have failed – not least because such things are only negatively in the gift of politicians and governments. That is, governments can do a great deal to mess things up, but rarely to improve things beyond their control. And so, it is best to offer only vague or misleading pledges which can be spun as successes even when everyone knows they were failures.

By the 1980s, neoliberal pretentions to free-markets and a small state provided even more leeway to politicians and corporate grafters alike. Where Wilson's attempt at a white-heat transformation had been administered by a government which actively managed the economy's critical infrastructure along with its banking system, Thatcher's botched attempt at an entrepreneurial revolution was placed in the hands of self-interested corporations which invariably engaged in rent-seeking rather than productive investment. Meanwhile, oil and gas from the North Sea intertwined with financial sector deregulation to generate the debt-based boom and bust presided over by Thatcher's illegitimate New Labour progeny.

In the years since the 2008 bust, graft is all that remains of the optimistic and outward looking great projects of the post-war boom. In the energy sector, nuclear fusion and renewable energy confidence tricks have been used to funnel billions of dollars, pounds and euros into the pockets of the financial sector overlords of the emerging corporatist economies of the west – the green energy technocrats and the Environmental, Social and Governance (ESG) fund management corporations get ever fatter on state handouts, while increasingly impoverished western populations are left to pick up the bill through higher taxes and cuts to public services. The same thing happened with the 2020-22 pandemic, only this time it was the pharmaceutical industry whose snout was in the state funding trough. More sordidly, in the UK, Tory ministers made no secret of the fact that they were shovelling pandemic funds at companies owned by family members, friends and donors. Meanwhile, government pandemic grants became a multi-billion-pound fraudsters' bonanza even as thousands of ordinary workers had to get by on £96 per week sick pay. And at the time of writing, it is the western armaments corporations which are being afforded a publicly funded jackpot as the NATO states send their old weapons to Ukraine to be captured or destroyed by the Russian military.

In the UK, where there used to be a nominally accountable government, we now have an unaccountable quasi-private project and service delivery arm made up of corporations like Serco, G4S, Capita and the now defunct Carillion, which oversee everything from hospital dinners to new toll roads. And as with the politicians who fund them, they prefer to avoid measurable and time bound performance targets for fear they will be found wanting.

The political class and their corporate paymasters have been playing this game for decades. And it seemed to work. So long as the population – or at least a large part of it – continued to enjoy rising living standards, the political class could go unchallenged. But then 2008 happened and the rotten edifice began to crumble.

Notes

1. *The difference between "can" and "can."* Tim Watkins, 16 October 2017. *Consciousness of Sheep* website. https://consciousnessofsheep.co.uk/2017/10/16/the-difference-between-can-and-can/

Technocracy for technocracy's sake

They called themselves "The Masters of the Universe." They were the central bankers who had finally conquered the cycles of boom and bust. By the beginning of the new century, with the recession of the 1980s and the collapse of the Soviet Union behind them, they had ushered in a "Great Moderation" in which the economy and wages grew in step with inflation at roughly two percent per year. Through the simple act of making miniscule changes to the overnight bank lending rate, they had been able to tame the economic volatility which had very nearly brought the western economies down in the 1970s.

They had stood like Gods looking down on the petty affairs of mere mortals. Then, seemingly out of nowhere, it all went wrong. As Charles Eisenstein was to put it in the wake of the crash[1]:

> "Money's divine property of abstraction, of disconnection from the real world of things, reached its extreme in the early years of the twenty-first century as the financial economy lost its mooring in the real economy and took on a life of its own. The vast fortunes of Wall Street were unconnected to any material production, seeming to exist in a separate realm.
>
> "Looking down from Olympian heights, the financiers called themselves 'masters of the universe,' channeling the power of the god they served to bring fortune or ruin upon the masses, to literally move mountains, raze forests, change the course of rivers, cause the rise and fall of nations. But money soon proved to be a capricious god. As I write these words, it seems that the increasingly frantic rituals that the financial priesthood uses to placate the god Money are in vain. Like the clergy of a dying

religion, they exhort their followers to greater sacrifices while blaming their misfortunes either on sin (greedy bankers, irresponsible consumers) or on the mysterious whims of God (the financial markets). But some are already blaming the priests themselves."

The Queen of England would later famously ask the clerisy at the London School of Economics, why nobody had seen it coming. To which the assembled luminaries could only bow their heads, shuffle their feet and murmur something about black swans. The Queen was misinformed though. It turned out later that plenty of people saw it coming, including contrarian economists like Steve Keen, whose modelling had shown that any reduction in *the rate of* borrowing was sufficient to trigger a cascading collapse of the heavily extended western banking and financial sector. And yet it was precisely curbing the rate of borrowing which the western central banks had been attempting to achieve since 2005 when prices had begun to tick up.

In this sense at least, the central bankers had been spectacularly successful. Not only had they encouraged us to stop borrowing, but they had also done so on such a scale that, had it not been for multi-state intervention and bailouts, there would have been no western banks left to borrow from. For millions of people in the real world though, the crash – and the depression which followed – was devastating. As Eisenstein put it:

> "What we call recession, an earlier culture might have called 'God abandoning the world.' Money is disappearing, and with it another property of spirit: the animating force of the human realm. At this writing, all over the world machines stand idle. Factories have ground to a halt; construction equipment sits derelict in the yard; parks and libraries are closing; and millions go homeless and hungry while housing units stand vacant and food rots in the warehouses. Yet all the human and

material inputs to build the houses, distribute the food, and run the factories still exist. It is rather something immaterial, that animating spirit, which has fled. What has fled is money. That is the only thing missing, so insubstantial (in the form of electrons in computers) that it can hardly be said to exist at all, yet so powerful that without it, human productivity grinds to a halt."

One might, perhaps, have wished that the Queen of England still possessed some residual feudal power which might have allowed her to have the whole cabal of central bankers and economists carted off to the Tower of London, with at least some of their number being beheaded for their sins. But the supreme irony of 2008 and its aftermath was that not only did they – with the exception of a few Icelandic bankers – escape punishment, but they were *put back in charge* to oversee the recovery.

How could it possibly be that nobody with the power of decision stopped to wonder whether some root and branch inquiry into what had just happened might be required before the people who had caused the problem were put in charge of cleaning up the mess? This is not a rhetorical question. The fact that nobody *in a position of power* sought to seriously question the established orthodoxy points to a fundamental flaw in western governance.

The economists and central bankers provide an example of the capture and perversion of an entire sector of knowledge and practice by a self-serving technocratic elite. As Steve Keen tried to warn[2], the "economics" taught in universities, learned and parroted by professional economists, and practiced by the central bankers, had no grounding in reality. But Keen ran into an invisible technocratic wall which prevents contrarians and non-economists from entering the hallowed halls of top-tier university economics departments, and which censored heresy and blasphemy from the official economics journals.

This is how it is done, of course. University departments are captured by the neoliberal insiders of their discipline. At the same time, journal editorial boards, beholden to their corporate owners, are taken over by neoliberal insiders. The result is that existing academics who refuse to toe the line are bullied out – often because their employment is dependent upon good journal reviews from journals who refuse to publish their work. And once this technocratic wall is in place, there is no chance for a contrarian to enter the new priesthood.

When the Queen of England, and, indeed, the economists themselves, talked about "nobody seeing it coming," what they meant was that nobody *on the inside* of that invisible technocratic wall could see it coming. They were the "experts" who Michael Gove attacked during his infamous Brexit interview in 2016. What most people missed – and what the technocratic establishment media wilfully ignores – is the second half of Gove's statement:

> "I think the people in this country have had enough of experts *from organisations with acronyms saying that they know what is best and getting it consistently wrong.*"

Time and again, organisations with acronyms and individuals with the right letters after their name, are afforded authority and status in almost inverse proportion to their results. And the problem is not limited to economics. Across the sciences, technocratic walls have been erected to the detriment of all of us. We witness this in the catastrophic collapse in disruptive science[3] – the sort of science which might just come up with a viable alternative to depleting fossil fuels, a monetary system which might be subject to democratic oversight, or various means of cleaning up centuries of industrial pollution without starving billions of people to death:

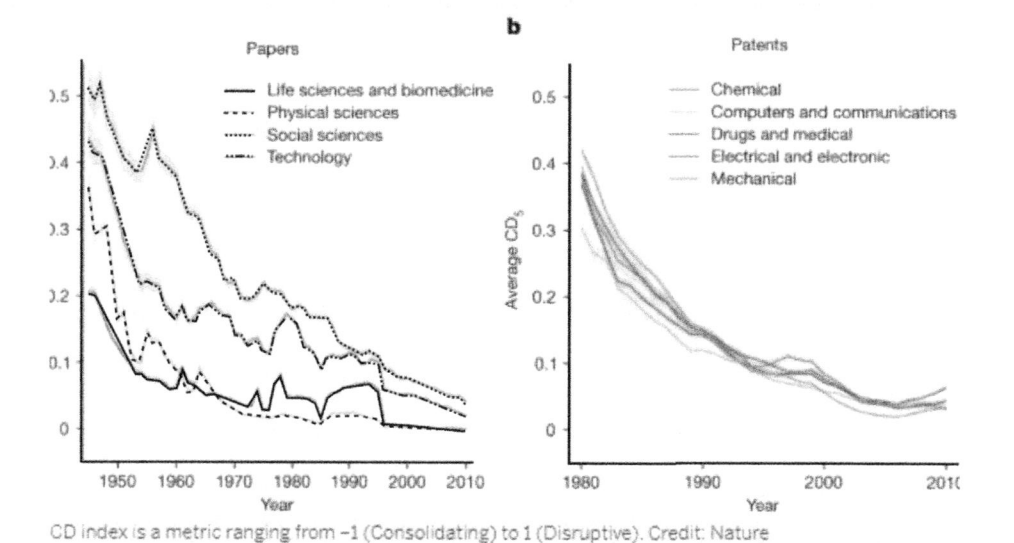

CD index is a metric ranging from −1 (Consolidating) to 1 (Disruptive). Credit: Nature

This decline is not just the result of diminishing returns as all of the easy research has been done, and each new project requires more people and vastly more funding to conduct. Indeed, the volume of research continues to grow. But as Rob Lownie at *UnHerd* explains[4]:

> "The findings... go against our expectations of scientific research as a process in which prior knowledge facilitates new discoveries, and where disciplines endlessly branch out into further sub-disciplines. Park, Leahy and Funk write that 'relative to earlier eras, recent papers and patents do less to push science and technology in new directions', and attribute the 'decline in disruptiveness to a narrowing in the use of previous knowledge'.
>
> "This is to say, a larger volume of material is being produced but scientific research is becoming increasingly specialised, to the point of esotericism and to the detriment of significant advances..."

It's the same invisible technocratic wall as we see in economics. "The Science" is reduced to only that science which appears in the official, peer reviewed journals...

37

journals long since captured by neoliberal corporations and edited by neoliberal zealots. Peer reviewed only by those firmly inside the technocratic wall. The entire process set up only to validate the existing orthodoxy and to exclude anything which smacks of heresy... that is, anything which might just be "disruptive." And so, at the very bottleneck moment when humanity desperately needs disruptive science to have even the slightest chance of getting to the other side largely unscathed, what passes for science is increasingly ossified. If only we had heeded the entirety of Eisenhower's military-industrial-congressional complex warning. But as with Michael Gove's experts quote, it is only remembered for the first part, raising the threat of the post-war USA becoming the military monster it had set out to slay[5]:

> "The total influence — economic, political, even spiritual — is felt in every city, every State house, every office of the Federal government. We recognize the imperative need for this development. Yet we must not fail to comprehend its grave implications. Our toil, resources and livelihood are all involved; so is the very structure of our society.
>
> "In the councils of government, we must guard against the acquisition of unwarranted influence, whether sought or unsought, by the military-industrial complex. The potential for the disastrous rise of misplaced power exists and will persist.
>
> "We must never let the weight of this combination endanger our liberties or democratic processes. We should take nothing for granted. Only an alert and knowledgeable citizenry can compel the proper meshing of the huge industrial and military machinery of defense with our peaceful methods and goals, so that security and liberty may prosper together."

Eisenhower's concerns were much broader, since even in the late 1950s, he had seen the growing threat that technocracy poses to a free and democratic society:

> "Akin to, and largely responsible for the sweeping changes in our industrial-military posture, has been the technological revolution during recent decades.
>
> "In this revolution, research has become central; it also becomes more formalized, complex, and costly. A steadily increasing share is conducted for, by, or at the direction of, the Federal government.
>
> "Today, the solitary inventor, tinkering in his shop, has been overshadowed by task forces of scientists in laboratories and testing fields. In the same fashion, the free university, historically the fountainhead of free ideas and scientific discovery, has experienced a revolution in the conduct of research. Partly because of the huge costs involved, a government contract becomes virtually a substitute for intellectual curiosity. For every old blackboard there are now hundreds of new electronic computers.
>
> "The prospect of domination of the nation's scholars by Federal employment, project allocations, and the power of money is ever present and is gravely to be regarded. Yet, in holding scientific research and discovery in respect, as we should, we must also be alert to the equal and opposite danger that public policy could itself become the captive of a scientific-technological elite."

The same kind of invisible technocratic wall that protects economists, generals and arms manufacturers had a dramatic impact on the response to the pandemic in 2020. "Trust the science" – literally the most unscientific statement anyone could make – was shorthand for "trust what the approved public health insiders are telling you." It didn't help though, that "the science" changed from moment to moment. In January 2020, it was considered racist to suggest that Covid-19 was dangerous. By April of 2020, as a disproportionate death rate among Black and Asian people was recorded, it became racist *not to* suggest that Covid-19 was dangerous. By then, public health experts were keen to tell us that masks don't prevent the spread of the virus. A year later, countries around the world had adopted mask mandates, obliging people to wear masks in public places and fining those who refused. In the longer-term, however, it is the narrow, public health-orientated composition of the pandemic technocracy which will prove to have wreaked the greatest damage. No thought was given to the long-term impacts on the economy of lockdown measures which were sold to a frightened public as the *only* defence against what turned out to be a relatively modest pandemic. And yet within days of the first UK lockdown in March 2020, the first – unlikely and unpredictable – supply chain disruption materialised in the he shape of an egg carton shortage. As is often the case with such disruptions, we – the public and the technocrats – only discovered after the event that there are just three egg carton manufacturers in Europe. And unfortunately for the UK, the nearest of these – in Denmark – was closed for a holiday.

The reason why egg cartons disappeared – and, incidentally, why there was a toilet paper shortage – was foreseeable though. It was the result of a rapid and unprepared switch from wholesale to retail demand brought about by the lockdowns. That is, in ordinary circumstances, the majority of eggs consumed in the UK are in the wholesale side of the economy – in restaurants, cafes, schools, hospitals, works canteens, etc. Because of the large numbers involved, these eggs are shipped in large trays of 30 or more eggs at a time. So that, as millions of people who would have ordinarily eaten in those wholesale-supplied outlets were suddenly forced to eat their eggs at home, demand for supermarket and shop eggs – which come in cartons of six or twelve – quickly outstripped supply. And because of the computerised systems operated by supermarkets, there was no mechanism to allow people to bring their own containers. And so, people went without eggs even as farmers were forced to throw eggs away.

Something similar happened with toilet roll. Again, the majority of toilet paper is consumed outside the home during the working day. Much of it in those giant rolls used in workplace and public toilets. So that, as millions of people used the toilet at home rather than at work, supplies began to run out. Soon enough, news of shortages fuelled additional demand. Not – as a sensationalist media would have you believe – because people began filling trolleys with toilet roll, but simply because each of us buying one additional roll is enough to overwhelm our just-in-time supply chains.

These early disruptions were relatively trivial compared to the shortages of fossil fuels, minerals and key components like computer chips which emerged when governments attempted to open up the *global* economy in the autumn of 2021. At the time of writing, a large part of the UK population is struggling to afford the rising price of electricity, gas, and petrol. Demand for used cars is high because of a shortage of new cars, which cannot be made for want of computer chips. The cost of shipping from Asia to the UK has risen four-fold due to supply chain disruption. And so, across the economy, businesses, faced with rising costs, are unable to reach a balance between the need to raise prices and the need to avoid deterring cash-strapped customers.

Labour shortages have materialised across the most affluent regions of the economy, even as unemployment and especially under-employment remain stubbornly high in the poorer regions. The three reasons for this appear to be, first, that younger workers took the opportunity of lockdown to re-train and seek better-paid work. Second, that low-paid migrant workers decided to return home to see out the pandemic. And third, that many – some estimates are as high as half a million – over-50s have used what pensions, property and savings they have to opt out of the workplace. The result is that thousands of low-paying businesses in the big cities and holiday resorts cannot attract the workers they need at wage rates that they can afford to pay.

Even in the cherished NHS which, supposedly, lockdowns were designed to protect, the long-term consequence of lockdowns is shaping up to be worse than unchecked Covid-19 would have been. Ordinary medical services were severely curtailed during the first lockdown, and never fully returned. Seeing a General Practitioner– the gateway to diagnostic and treatment services – face-to-face was all but impossible. And with hospitals reportedly overrun with Covid sufferers, few were in a hurry to call for an ambulance or go to an Accident and Emergency department, even when they needed to.

One consequence, when lockdowns came to an end, was that the NHS was unable to cope with pent-up demand from people who had lived with their symptoms for months if not years. By the autumn of 2021, hospitals across the UK were unable to treat the volume of people turning up with emergencies like heart attacks, strokes, and broken bones. Ambulance queues outside hospitals became so great that what remains of the British Army had to be drafted in to drive ambulances on non-emergency calls. Worse still, many of those turning up had conditions – like cancers – which might have been easier – and cheaper – to treat if diagnosed early, but which now required more intensive, potentially less successful, and often more expensive courses of treatment. Many more face long-term limitation and disability for conditions which ought to have been easily treated if only the NHS had been operating normally.

NHS staff have also paid a high price for lockdown. Exposed to Covid on a daily basis, the death rate among frontline health workers – particularly in the early days when we had a shortage of protective equipment – was far higher than any other workplace. And even among those fortunate enough not to die, incidences of long-covid are high and enduring. More broadly, those not directly involved in the treatment of covid risked burn-out as they attempted to continue treating the full range of conditions while having to follow restrictive covid safety precautions. The end result is a far smaller workforce facing far greater demands as the number of people waiting for treatment and surgery spirals upward. All else being equal – which, as we will see, it isn't – it will be a decade or more before staffing levels and waiting times return to their pre-covid levels.

As attention turns toward the post-covid inquiries, the government line – many would say "lie" – is that "we were only following the science." But even if this were true, the "science" that they were purporting to follow was a technocratic insider anti-science which dismissed as heresy any scientists who put forward alternative approaches to the management of Covid. When the full economic costs of lockdown are finally totted-up and the lockdown balance sheet made available, it might well be that the many scientists behind the Great Barrington approach – which suggested protecting the vulnerable while the virus spread, relatively painlessly through the wider, and particularly the younger population – will be proved correct.

The issue that is bound to be raised – and likely dismissed – during the inquiries into the pandemic is whether and to what extent the technocrats *conspired* to make things pan out the way they did. There were, no doubt, conspiracies within the technocracy. For example, the publication of Dr Anthony Fauci's e-mails under USA freedom of information rules, confirms that at the beginning of the pandemic senior scientists from both sides of the Atlantic believed, and wished to cover up, the probability that SARS-CoV-2 had escaped from a laboratory. It is also clear that the same scientists coordinated a response from leading virologists to claim that the lab-leak story was a "conspiracy theory." In some quarters, this collusion has been interpreted as evidence that these people were involved in some kind of grand conspiracy to unleash the pandemic and then to benefit from its consequences. And while this cannot be ruled out entirely, a more likely explanation is the usual defensiveness within technocratic silos. These, after all, were scientists living and working within the very narrow invisible technocratic wall of international virology and various forms of gain of function research. Even the possibility of a lab leak would threaten millions or even billions of dollars' worth of research grants. And so, SARS-CoV-2 simply had to have natural origins... even though, as former *Economist* science editor Matt Ridley argues[6], no evidence for the natural evolution of the virus has ever been presented.

The idea that something as noble as scientific enquiry might be corrupted by something as base as money is anathema to most people. And yet, everywhere we look we find technocrats using the invisible walls to deflect attention away from straightforward robbery. As Malcom Kyeyune puts it[7]:

> "Kings ruled in the epoch of monarchies, because only kings could rule, or at least so they all claimed... And just like the kings of old, our technocrats at one point claimed (and even enjoyed) a form of quasi-magical power in the eyes of their peasantry; a view once commonly shared that they could use the very thing that made them rightful rulers – science, logic, rationality, data – to lay on hands, cure ills, and improve society.

> "Put plainly: managers, through the power of managerialism, were once believed to be able to mobilize science and reason and progress to accomplish what everyone else could not, and so only they could secure a just and functional society for their subjects, just as only the rightful kings of yore could count on Providence and God to do the same thing. At their core, both of these claims are truly metaphysical, because all claims to legitimate rulership are metaphysical. It is when that metaphysical power of persuasion is lost that kings or socialists become 'bourgeois'... They have to desperately turn toward *providing proof*, because the genuine belief is gone. But once a spouse starts demanding that the other spouse constantly prove that he or she hasn't been cheating, the marriage is already over, and the divorce is merely a matter of time..."

Whenever a spotlight is turned on one or other silo within the technocracy, graft and penny pinching always comes to the fore. The only truly remarkable issue being the degree of wilful blindness on the part of those paid by the technocracy, who take the money while turning a blind eye to the corruption. Consider convicted fraudster Elizabeth Holmes. Once lauded as America's first female tech billionaire and likened to figures like Apple's Steve Jobs and Tesla's Elon Musk, Holmes conned some of America's richest and most powerful men – including media proprietor Rupert Murdoch, former President Bill Clinton, and former statesmen George Schultz and Henry Kissinger – into backing a fake technology – a machine that could supposedly replace medical blood tests. At one point, Holmes' company, Theranos was valued at over $9bn. But despite *having to know* that the technology could not work, the scientists and technicians who worked for Theranos took the money and looked the other way. It was only when an anonymous whistle-blower was persuaded to provide evidence to Wall Street Journal reporter John Carreyrou, that things began to unravel. Even then, it took a further five years before the authorities finally brought fraud charges against Holmes.

Widespread wilful blindness is another of those things which most members of the public refuse to acknowledge. One of the arguments raised in relation to both real and imagined conspiracies, is that with so many people involved, someone would be bound to blow the whistle. But all too often, nobody does. Consider, for example, the hundreds of people who were involved in decrypting German Enigma signals at Bletchley Park during the Second World War. It was only when Tory MP Rupert Allason – writing under the pen name Nigel West in the early 1980s – began alluding to the fact that a large part of what had been assumed to be allied military expertise may have owed more to simply reading the enemy's intentions and dispositions, that people who had worked at Bletchley Park began to talk publicly about their work.

The former cryptologists who kept Bletchley Park's activities secret did so largely for noble motives – bolstered no doubt by the terms of the Official Secrets Act – since one way or another the activities would have continued throughout the Cold War. More often though, it is base money that explains why so many of us choose to look the other way. As Margaret Heffernan cautions[8]:

> "Money does influence us and it does make us feel better. That's why companies pay overtime and bonuses. It may not, in and of itself, make us absolutely happy – but, just like cigarettes and chocolate, our wants are not confined to what's good for us. The pleasure of money is often short-lived of course – because it's insatiable. There are always newer, bigger, flashier, sweeter products to consume, so the things we buy with money rarely satisfy as fully as they promise. Psychologists call this the hedonic treadmill: the more we consume, the more we want. But we stay on the treadmill as steadfastly as on

our phones, hooked on the pleasures that, at least initially, make us feel so good.

"What all this has shown is that money may be the richest area ever discovered for the study of unintended consequences. From which it should follow, but rarely does, that managers and compensation committees need to be tremendously thoughtful when deciding how to apply such a powerful, even irrational, motivator. Because money has a more complex influence on people than just making them work longer."

Heffernan's example of W.R. Grace, the main employer in Libby, Montana is instructive in showing just how far people will go to turn a blind eye when their future income depends upon it. Grace was an asbestos mining company whose activities led to the entire town being dusted with microscopic asbestos fibres to the point that the local death rate was three times higher than average. Yet for years nobody blew the whistle, even when they had to watch loved ones dying as a result. And when local resident Gayla Benefield spoke out, far from public support and relief, she was met with hostility and hate mail.

This, perhaps, is also why nobody inside nuclear fusion's technocratic invisible wall came out to set the record straight about mendacious claims made to the US Congress, the EU Commission and the UK Parliament that the next generation of fusion reactors would provide 500 units of energy for every 50 units fed in. A ten to one energy return on energy invested would certainly make nuclear fusion commercially viable – not least because once commercial investment is secured, a raft of relatively low-cost efficiency savings and economies of scale would likely boost the energy return on energy invested to a point where fusion could overtake fission and renewables as an alternative to fossil fuels... except... except that the 500 to 50 data was deliberately misrepresented by a technocracy which depends entirely upon state funding for its existence. As investigative journalist Steven B. Krivit explains[9], the fusion technocracy has consistently obfuscated the difference between the *thermal* energy in the fusion reaction and the *total* energy required to operate the various reactors – the energy out is heat not electricity and even if 100 percent of the heat could be converted into electricity, this would still not be enough to power the reactor:

> "In a 1993 hearing, nuclear fusion research representatives convinced the U.S. Congress to spend public money on ITER, the International Thermonuclear Experimental Reactor. ITER, they said, was the way to fusion energy. Elected officials in Europe, Japan, and the [former] Soviet Union also agreed to fund ITER. Later, China, India, and South Korea joined the partnership. The revised estimated cost, including parts, is now $65 billion.
>
> "For experimental evidence of progress, the representatives implied that, in 1997, the Joint European Torus (JET) fusion reactor produced thermal power from fusion at a rate of 66 percent of the total reactor input power. That foundation, as it turns out, was flawed. The power produced by JET was only 1 percent of the total reactor input power.
>
> "With this false foundation, they proposed the ITER reactor, which, they implied, would produce ten times the power it would consume. This promise was also flawed. If ITER works as planned, the overall reactor will produce power at the same rate as it consumes power. Although this result would accomplish its scientific objective — a tenfold gain of plasma heating power — the overall reactor output will be equivalent to a zero net-power reactor.
>
> "Fusion representatives told Congress, the public, and the news media that the ITER reactor would produce

'500 megawatts of fusion power' and that it would prove that fusion on Earth is commercially viable. These false impressions took root decades ago and, by 2017, had been established as apparent fact as shown in records from the European Commission, European Parliament, U.S. Congress, fusion industry partners, educational organizations, and news organizations."

From solar roadways to hyperloops and from seabed mining to Mars colonies, we witness billions of dollars, euros and pounds being squandered on technological scams fronted up by modern day "green" P.T. Barnums. The more outlandish the claim, and the more charismatic the salesman, the more an establishment media wedded to the religion of progress loses any grounding it may have had in reality. It falls to citizen journalists and disinterested engineers and physicists to – relatively easily – debunk the graft which establishment outlets cannot bring themselves to acknowledge. Even here, the social media platforms which once allowed citizen journalists to raise issues of concern are increasingly censored, with those on the outside of the various technocratic silos de-platformed or shadow-banned by algorithms programmed to give more weight to pontificating insiders than to actual *evidence* presented by those outside the technocratic wall.

The role of the establishment media and, increasingly, social media in setting the "Overton window" for what constitutes acceptable v unacceptable science, points to another invisible technocratic wall which those cast as outsiders cannot break through. This though, has proved far more difficult to enforce in an age of information-overload and activist journalism. Unlike professions such as medicine or law, there is no protected status for journalism. In an age where almost every household in the developed western states has access to word-processing technology, anyone can be a journalist – albeit that most would be very poor journalists, and many would be unable to separate what is happening from what they *wish* was happening.

The term "legacy media" has been used to describe the old, hierarchical news organisations which dominated the information landscape as recently as 15 years ago. Even with the arrival of the internet and the first hobby bloggers, it was only after the development of social media toward the end of the first decade of the century, that the reputation of the old establishment media outlets came under fire. The main reason for this is that while news organisations claimed to deal in facts, in reality they dealt in *narratives*.

In an earlier age, one might have turned to activist newspapers such as the *Morning Star* or the *Socialist Worker* to find the facts that the establishment media had omitted from their narrative. In the same manner, at the height of the Cold War, insomniacs tuned in to *Radio Moscow* to get a different take on such things as the deployment of American cruise missiles in the UK. But these were a tiny minority of readers and listeners. The overwhelming majority derived their news from a handful of – mostly neoliberal-leaning – newspapers, four television channels, and a handful of radio stations. So that, even if people *felt* that there was something wrong with the official narrative, they had few alternative sources of facts and data with which to make a challenge.

Go back even further, to Good Friday 1930, when there was just one UK news broadcaster – the embryonic British Broadcasting Corporation – and listeners tuning in to the 8.45pm news bulletin were told that "there is no news tonight." Instead, they were treated to 15 minutes of piano music. Not, of course, that nothing had happened. A massive storm had wrought destruction in the Philippines, Indian nationalists had seized an armoury in Chittagong, causing the British to declare martial law, and a fire in a church in Romania had killed 118 people. It is inconceivable that, in today's age of 24-hour news, such events would not be reported. But in those early days, authority was used to mask inadequacy.

The early BBC was far smaller than today's lumbering dinosaur. While it may have had an India desk, it is doubtful it would have had a reporter on the ground in Chittagong. It likely didn't have reporters on the ground in the Philippines or Romania. And even if it had, this being Good Friday, those reporters would likely have been on holiday anyway. To a large degree, then, "news" meant only that news that occurred where there were reporters on the ground. Reporters, in turn, were only on the ground in places which reflected the news outlet's priorities. In the sprawling British Empire of the inter-war years, home news trumped news from the colonies and dominions, while these trumped news from countries and regions outside the empire.

Television made the problem worst because of the additional costs involved. The BBC produced its first outside broadcast in 1937, covering the coronation of King George VI. But it would not be until the late 1960s that outside broadcasting became more commonplace, particularly with the flagship *Nationwide* programme which drew together reports from the UK regions every evening. In the USA, television had developed much earlier, but the same cost issues put similar limitations on the breadth of coverage. As in the UK, American broadcasters discovered the paradox of scarcity. As Martin Gurri explains[10]:

> "A curious thing happens to sources of information under conditions of scarcity. They become authoritative. A century ago, a scholar wishing to study the topics under public discussion in the US would find most of them in the pages of the New York Times. It wasn't quite 'All the news that's fit to print,' but it delivered a large enough

proportion of published topics that, as a practical proposition, little incentive existed to look further. Because it held a near monopoly on current information, the New York Times seemed authoritative.

"Four decades ago, Walter Cronkite concluded his broadcasts of the CBS Nightly News with the words, 'And that's the way it was.' Few of his viewers found it extraordinary that the clash and turmoil of billions of human lives, dwelling in thousands of cities and organized into dozens of nations, could be captured in three or four mostly visual reports lasting a total of less than 30 minutes. They had no access to what was missing—the other two networks reported the same news, only less majestically."

Scarcity also allowed for the growth of hierarchical news organisations funded by advertising, and with little in the way of competition. Just as viewers, listeners and readers had no alternative outlets, so advertisers had no alternative means of reaching their customer base. The benefit of this was that news organisations could afford to pay the salaries and expenses of top-tier investigative journalists. The downside was that well-financed news organisations had undue influence on the affairs of state – sometimes legitimately, as in the case of the Watergate investigation, but more often illegitimately, as in the *Sun's* coverage of the Hillsborough disaster, or its boast that it had aided Tony Blair's victory in the 1997 general election.

In theory, news outlets had been accountable to state regulators. They could also be exposed by citizen researchers. But crucially, by the time some correction or apology was made, the original narrative had been fixed in the public mind. It took more than a quarter of a century, for example, to secure the inquiries into Hillsborough and the Bloody Sunday murders, which eventually set the record straight and obliged news outlets and government agencies to make belated apologies. But this was always too little, too late.

What the bad behaviour of news organisations did achieve, in drip-drip fashion, was the gradual undermining of public trust. So that when, in 2011, the tabloid press was exposed for illegally hacking people's phones – most notoriously leaving a message on the phone of murdered schoolgirl Milly Dowler, sending the police on a wild goose chase and giving her distraught parents the false hope that she was still alive – the result was a major public backlash and a yet-to-be-resolved call for better regulation.

By then though, those same mobile phones were taking their own toll on legacy news organisations that were well past their sell-by date. The first Apple i-phone had arrived in January 2007. The evolution toward the smartphones of today followed in short order. By 2011, it was possible to record TV quality footage on a hand-held phone. And with the advent of social media, citizen and activist journalists had the means of directly disseminating their work without the need to filter it through an existing news site.

The impact, however, was largely negative. That is, while some notable independent journalists and online news outlets have emerged, the main impact of mobile phones and social media was to provide *instant rebuttal* of the official narrative expounded by the establishment media. When campaigning academic Phil Scraton refused to let go of the injustice of Hillsborough, it took him years to get access to police and legal information deposited in the House of Lords library. And when he finally got access, he was forbidden to use a camera or photocopier. Instead, he had to make his own copies using a pencil and paper. Today, much of that information would have been available online and – assuming one was granted or otherwise obtained the password – could be accessed with a few mouse clicks. It is the same for just about any story or issue. For example, I have found it easy to debunk the *Guardian's* pro-green energy coverage by simple reference to the Ofgem (the energy sector regulator) website, where monthly energy generation data is readily available. And for the record, no, there has *never* been a day when the UK has run entirely on renewable energy.

Politically contentious issues continue to be problematic for establishment news outlets which invariably report from behind the official lines. For example, news organisations have a long history of entanglement with police – and, perhaps more worryingly, with security services – because their work often overlaps. A good reporter may refuse to give up a source, but they might suggest that the police look into the activities of certain local villains. In return, while the police officer may not disclose police operations, they might suggest that a reporter might want to be at a certain location at a certain time. Such trade-offs lead to a degree of trust of police which may well bias reporting – as it did with Hillsborough, but also as it did with such contentious protests as the picketing of the coking plant at Orgreave in 1984 or the anti-poll tax demonstration in London in March 1990.

In the latter case, we got a taste of things to come. Early hand-held video recorders were becoming more common by 1990. And while most of the people who attended the poll tax demonstration had no way of recording events, a significant minority did. Although individual footage was not particularly useful, an appeal for copies of time stamped footage allowed documentary makers to produce a programme for Channel 4 – *The Battle of Trafalgar* – which showed the policing of the demonstration in a very different light to that portrayed by the establishment media. Agent provocateurs were exposed, so too were police actions which prevented people from escaping the horse charge in Whitehall and the police vehicles driven at speed into the crowds in an overcrowded Trafalgar Square – the event which triggered the rioting which the establishment media used to give the impression that this was some form of insurrection.

Today, all of that police misbehaviour would have been recorded and distributed in real time by an army of people using smartphones. By now though, cost pressures have turned most establishment news outlets into shadows of their former selves.

Social media gave advertisers a means of targeting and focussing their advertising in a way that establishment outlets could only dream of. Newspaper advertising, and even more so TV, was scattergun in nature. An advertiser could, to some extent, work out which papers or programmes would reach their target audience. But their adverts would inevitably reach a much wider audience than they would have liked. From an early stage, software developers began creating programmes and algorithms which understood our spending habits better than we did. Famously, Tesco's computerised customer loyalty system prompted them to send a "congratulations on your pregnancy" card to a customer who didn't yet realise that she was pregnant. By the time social media arrived, these programmes had developed to the point that they allowed advertisers to home in on their precise customer base. Better still, tracking cookies allowed the advertiser to 'follow' those who had shown an interest as they surfed the web from site to site. At the same time, competing advertisers could use these tracking cookies to target people who had responded to a competitor's advertising.

As online advertising flourished, so traditional advertising atrophied. News was the first casualty. The days when local newspapers could employ several investigative reporters to formally report on local stories, and informally to act as a training ground and a pool of skilled labour for the national news outlets, are long behind us. With a handful of exceptions, "local" news outlets are merely branch offices for national and international organisations whose only contribution to news is to copy and reproduce press releases from local authorities and approved local lobby groups. Even the national outlets struggle to afford a large complement of reporters, preferring instead to use commentary to fill the space that would previously have been taken up with genuine investigative reporting.

Audiences have responded accordingly, switching away from physical newsprint and television news in favour of the social media feed. The complaint from the establishment media outlets is that online news sources are unreliable, biased, and in some cases entirely fake. It is a charge that might garner more support but for the fact that the same charges can reasonably be levied against the establishment media themselves these days.

The rot goes all the way back to the origins of the establishment media, with debates between such luminaries as Walter Lippmann and John Dewey over what, exactly, was the purpose of news. As Christopher Lasch explains[11]:

> "The role of the press, as Lippmann saw it, was to circulate information, not to encourage argument. The relationship between information and argument was antagonistic, not complementary. He did not take the position that reliable information was a necessary precondition of argument; on the contrary, his point was that information precluded argument, made argument unnecessary. Arguments were what took place in the absence of reliable information. Lippmann had forgotten what he learned (or should have learned) from William James and John Dewey: that our search for reliable information is itself guided by the questions that arise during arguments about a given course of action. It is only by subjecting our preferences and projects to the

test of debate that we come to understand what we know and what we still need to learn."

Lippmann's side won that argument, with mass media claiming to be above the political and ideological fray. Merely presenting the facts as they occurred. Although, as critics have pointed out down the ages, the "facts" that were presented fitted into a narrow window of what was perceived to be mainstream opinion but which all too often turned out to be only the range of opinions found acceptable by advertisers and proprietors.

A combination of recruitment policy and wilful blindness over decades has ensured that newsrooms are filled with people who dismiss out of hand any idea or perspective that falls outside the window of technocratic acceptability. In a famous exchange between Noam Chomsky and BBC journalist Andrew Marr, Marr objected that he never felt pressured to bend his opinions to fit those of the BBC. Chomsky countered that this may well be true, but if Marr didn't have the opinions he had, he wouldn't be sat where he was. In this way, those involved in the production of news are able to convince themselves that theirs is a purely objective and factual account of the world.

The world view which establishment media operate within is *neoliberal* and *globalist* in nature. It is a view which depends upon an unconscious mish-mash of Orwellian double-speak to describe a world which is radically different to the description itself. For example, it speaks about the primacy of "free markets," and is vehemently opposed to direct state intervention despite the reality that the "market" is controlled by a relative handful of oligarchs and massive, faceless corporations like Black Rock – all of whom depend upon state handouts and friendly legislation to remain profitable and powerful. It is a world view of a university educated technocracy which is no longer tied to place – a metropolitan liberalism which can ease comfortably from one global city to another. As such, it rejects the idea that charity should begin at home; seeing little difference between the poor in the run down cities of its own country and the impoverished masses of the third world.

Perhaps it was ever thus. In *Bleak House* – published in 20 episodes in 1852-53 – Dickens referred to it as "telescopic philanthropy" – Mrs Jellyby spends her time working to improve the plight of the people of Borrioboola-Gha, on the left bank of the Niger river, while her own neglected children are left to fend for themselves. It is the same "white man's burden" that today manifests in the form of white, university-educated metropolitan neoliberals seeking to improve the lot of racial and religious minorities by casting them in the role of eternal victims. It is the world view which can simultaneously call for open borders and state support for economic migrants while dismissing the indigenous poor as chavs and scroungers.

By ignoring the key issues of class and place, this neoliberal media window of acceptability sets up a fake continuum from left to right in which only the neoliberal centre – left and right – political views are deemed acceptable. In this way, the supposedly extreme views of John McDonnell and Jeremy Corbyn, together with the supposedly hard right views of Nigel Farage are excluded or derided. And the fact that organisations like the BBC receive complaints from both left and right is held up as evidence that they are balanced. The terminology of "left" and "right" though – stemming from the seating arrangements in the eighteenth-century revolutionary French Assembly, the left being anti- and the right pro-monarchy – obscures more than it explains in the modern world. If, instead of left v right, we juxtapose axes such as nationalist v globalist, social liberal v social conservative, authoritarian v libertarian, economic liberalism v economic interventionism, we develop a far more grounded view of the complexity of our current politics. The UK Labour and Conservative Parties – like the US Republican and Democrat parties – are both neoliberal since they promote group-based social and economic individualism. So that while there is plenty of scope for heated arguments between the two – for example over tax and spending policy – there is no question of their stepping outside the window of acceptability – for example by seeking to redistribute wealth, to nationalise critical infrastructure or even to think of limiting private banks' ability to print currency out of thin air. Other parties and viewpoints are far less easy to pigeon-hole. Britain's Social Democratic Party (SDP) for example, is widely believed to be on the extreme right because of its conservative views on family, community, and nation. On economic issues though, the SDP is in favour of nationalisation and redistribution policies to the left of those pursued by McDonnell in the run up to the 2017 general election. In a similar vein, Libertarians are considered to be on the extreme right as a result of their support for free markets. But on social issues such as abortion, most take what is considered the left-wing view that the state should not interfere with a woman's right to choose. In this sense, complaints against the BBC from Labour and Conservative politicians and activists are not coming from opposite ends of the same axis but are often at right angles – the left criticising the BBC's *economic* neoliberal bias, Conservatives criticising the BBC's *social* neoliberalism.

This hegemony of the extreme centre[12] – "It strikes me that what's called the moderates are the most immoderate people possible" – leaves electorates with no practical alternative to the raft of problems which have been growing in strength and urgency since the late 1970s, and which have been accelerated by the 2008 crash and more recently by the Covid lockdowns and the response to the Russian invasion of Ukraine. Where previously opposition parties would offer an alternative vision of the future which might plausibly overcome or at least mitigate our growing list of woes, "insofar as the neoliberal parties have a vision it is to have no vision at all". Under the leadership of Kier "Keith" Starmer in the UK for example, the entire opposition could be replaced with a notice saying that "we would do the same as the government only more/better/faster."

The cosy neoliberal consensus among the political class does, however, open the way for a host of chancers and ne'er do wells to enter the political fray as rebel rousers. And so long as these "populist" leaders *appear* to be outsiders and *appear* to offer an alternative, they can rally a large degree of public support. But the moment they are revealed as political insiders – such as Jeremy Corbyn or more recently Boris Johnson ended up being – the support dissipates. Even Donald Trump's – allegedly civilisation-threatening – brief attempt to "make America Great again" ended up with Obama's Vice President and George Bush's neocon "crazies in the basement" returning to office in January 2021 and picking up where they left off in 2016 as if nothing had happened.

Meanwhile, and apparently beyond the understanding of the technocracy, the economic consequences of disrupted supply chains, locked-in commodity production and a lack of investment in new energy capacity is threatening to unleash a stagflationary crisis far worse than the 1970s, and possibly worse than any of the previous economic crises of the industrial age. At the time of writing, energy prices have risen far beyond what is affordable to the majority of the population. General price increases are crushing *discretionary* spending power from the economy. Food shortages are threatened – and even if absolute shortages fail to materialise, the rising price of food will plunge millions more households across the western economies into poverty.

And yet, despite the gravity of the situation, there is not a single competent leader in the western states. Worse still, there are no obvious leaders among the political class as a whole to replace the current crop of ne'er-do-wells thrown up by our hollowed-out and self-replicating neoliberal electoral systems. It is for this reason that we are forced to conclude that the problem here is structural rather than merely the coincidence that some 25 percent of the world's leading nations just happened to throw up incompetent and inadequate leader personalities all at the same time.

The issue at hand is, are we, as Martin Gurri argues, trapped somewhere between a new system waiting to be born and an old system which refuses to die? Or might Margaret Thatcher have been correct when she proclaimed that "there is no alternative?" Perhaps the unravelling of western civilisation is now inevitable.

Notes

1. Eisenstein, C. 2011. *Sacred Economics: Money, Gift, and Society in the Age of Transition*

2. Keen, S. 2011. *Debunking Economics - Revised and Expanded Edition: The Naked Emperor Dethroned?*

3. Park, M., Leahey, E. & Funk, R.J. Papers and patents are becoming less disruptive over time. Nature 613, 138–144 (2023). https://doi.org/10.1038/s41586-022-05543-x

4. Lownie, R. 5 January 2023. "Study finds science is becoming less innovative." *UnHerd*. https://unherd.com/thepost/study-finds-science-is-becoming-less-innovative

5. Military-Industrial Complex Speech, Dwight D. Eisenhower, 1961 - https://avalon.law.yale.edu/20th_century/eisenhower001.asp

6. Chan, A. and Ridley, M. 2021. *Viral: The Search for the Origin of Covid-19*

7. Kyeyune, M. 16 August 2021. "Farewell to Bourgeois Kings." https://tinkzorg.wordpress.com/2021/08/16/farewell-to-bourgeois-kings

8. Heffernan, M. *Wilful Blindness* (p. 219). Simon & Schuster UK

9. Krivit, S. 2021. *ITER, The Grand Illusion: A Forensic Investigation of Power Claims* https://youtu.be/xnikAFWDhNw or https://vimeo.com/535571108?embedded=true&source=video_title&owner=137465510

10. Gurri, M. 2016. *The Revolt of The Public and the Crisis of Authority in the New Millennium* (p. 20). Stripe Press. Kindle Edition.

11. Lasch, Christopher. 1997. *The Revolt of the Elites and the Betrayal of Democracy* (p. 170). W. W. Norton & Company.

12. David Graeber, 2021. Double Down News. https://youtu.be/-9afwZON8dU

Designed to fail

Inflation was the overarching concern of the 1970s. A basket of goods that might have been bought for £100 immediately after World War Two cost £279 in 1970 but had risen to £515 by 1975. By the time Margaret Thatcher had been elected in 1979, our basket of goods had risen to £853. And while the annual *rate* of inflation began to fall from a high point of 18 percent in 1980, inflation remained high until the middle of the decade – falling from six percent in 1983 to 3.5 percent in 1984, after which it began rising again, reaching 9.5 percent in 1990, by which time our post war basket of goods cost a staggering £1,899.

The myth that emerged in the 1970s was that inflation was caused by profligate governments caving in to demands from the electorate, and especially from over-powerful trades unions, and printing money out of thin air to pay for wage rises, welfare benefits and public services. In large part, this was believed to be the result of the policy of full employment pursued by western governments in the aftermath of the war. As Polish economist Michael Kalecki had pointed out as early as 1943[1], full employment results in serious "labour discipline" problems, as traditional incentives such as higher pay, lower hours and bonuses become subject to competition between employers, even as traditional sanctions hold less sway:

> "Indeed, under a regime of permanent full employment, the 'sack' would cease to play its role as a disciplinary measure. The social position of the boss would be undermined, and the self-assurance and class-consciousness of the working class would grow. Strikes for wage increases and improvements in conditions of work would create political tension. It is true that profits would be higher under a regime of full employment than they are on the average under laissez-faire; and even the rise in wage rates resulting from the stronger bargaining

power of the workers is less likely to reduce profits than to increase prices, and thus adversely affects only the rentier interests..."

Kalecki also glimpsed the likely reaction when the in-built inflationary pressure reached a crisis point:

"In the slump, either under the pressure of the masses, or even without it, public investment financed by borrowing will be undertaken to prevent large-scale unemployment. But if attempts are made to apply this method in order to maintain the high level of employment reached in the subsequent boom, strong opposition by business leaders is likely to be encountered. As has already been argued, lasting full employment is not at all to their liking. The workers would 'get out of hand' and the 'captains of industry' would be anxious to 'teach them a lesson'. Moreover, the price increase in the upswing is to the disadvantage of small and big rentiers, and makes them 'boom-tired'.

"In this situation a powerful alliance is likely to be formed between big business and rentier interests, and they would probably find more than one economist to declare that the situation was manifestly unsound. The pressure of all these forces, and in particular of big business—as a rule influential in government departments—would most probably induce the government to return to the orthodox policy of cutting down the budget deficit..."

This was the advice eventually offered by a new school of "monetarist" economists, whose views had been forged out of the 1924 German hyperinflation and the political extremism which followed. Economists like Hayek and Friedman made the somewhat banal, and misleading[2] case that "inflation is everywhere and always a monetary phenomenon." Faced by growing inflation in the 1970s, politicians on all sides reached for the prescriptions offered by the monetarists to resolve their growing crises.

64

Limiting the amount *and* velocity of money in circulation, both by raising interest rates and by running a large government surplus, was intended to engineer precisely the kind of slump envisaged by Kalecki. And with an end to the commitment to maintaining full employment, government could embark on the process of dismantling the basis of trade union power... the loss of the economy's productive base being considered a price worth paying.

The received narrative is that it was only with the election of Margaret Thatcher in May 1979, and Ronald Reagan in 1980, that the western states could embark upon a monetarist (nascent neoliberal) revolution, based around a minimalist state, economic liberalism and increased international trade and finance. This though, overlooks earlier attempts to introduce the same programme of reform. In the UK, for example, the 1970-1974 government of Edward Heath attempted, but failed, to introduce monetarist reforms. Heath was defeated as much by the old guard of his own Conservative Party as by the massed ranks of the trades unions which played a large part in his downfall in February 1974. Harold Wilson fared no better at maintaining the post-war consensus and was replaced in 1976 by his monetarist-leaning Foreign Secretary, James Callaghan. Callaghan's speech at the 1976 Labour Party conference paved the way for a radical departure from the old order:

> "We used to think that you could spend your way out of a recession and increase employment by cutting taxes and boosting government spending. I tell you in all candour that that option no longer exists."

The speech was intended to give cover for a decision to use an International Monetary Fund (IMF) loan as an external constraint on future government spending. As Colin Thain and Maurice Wright explain[3]:

> "Callaghan's famous 'monetarist' speech to the Labour Party Conference was a tactical political attempt to achieve multiple objectives: to appease the financial markets, to frighten the Labour Party into accepting the need for tough measures, and to make the right impression on the US Treasury Secretary whose support would be vital for the UK to obtain IMF support."

The myth at the time was that a loan from the IMF was necessary to prevent the UK from being bankrupted. However, given that a sovereign state may print as much currency as it chooses, bankruptcy was not a possibility. Rather, the question was whether further money printing would so deter foreign investment that the value of the UK pound would collapse, forcing a period of "import substitution" onto an already crisis-riven economy. Callaghan and his Chancellor, Denis Healey, had no intention of finding out.

The IMF loan was agreed, along with a package of austerity cuts and an end to the policy of full employment, in December 1976 – although the political nature of the loan was to be evidenced by the fact that by 1979, less than half of the loan had been spent. What Callaghan and Healey had done, however, was to lay the foundations for Thatcher's revolution.

By May of 1979, the British electorate was changing too. The large baby boomer generation were young adults, struggling to find paid work, adequate housing and to raise families. And unlike their parents and grandparents, the boomers had no direct experience of war or of the economic depression and political extremism of the inter-war years. Like the youth of any age, the boomers felt constrained by the old order, and were more willing to take risks in exchange for the promise of brighter days ahead. It was this generation more than most that Thatcher appealed to.

To older folk who had lived through depression and war, only to face housing shortages and ongoing rationing in the immediate post-war years, social housing had been a godsend. But to a younger generation, social housing managed – and more often mismanaged – by bureaucratic local housing departments was stifling. Thatcher's promise of a new, "home-owning democracy" offered a radical change of direction to younger voters determined to improve their lot. Nor was it only housing which was mired in bureaucracy. Even something as modest as having a telephone installed was a chore in a system where both the line and the equipment had to be rented from a Post Office bureaucracy which moved at a snail's pace. Again, Thatcher's promise to open the economy to competition and to sweep away the red tape had huge appeal to Britain's younger voters.

Even Callaghan's apparent failure to get a grip on the economy – as demonstrated by the "winter of discontent" 1978-79 in which low paid workers across the economy came out on strike for higher pay – played into Thatcher's hands. Her claim being that Labour had lacked the courage to go *far enough* in its implementation of monetarist policy. It is from such seeds that her later reputation as "The Iron Lady" was to grow. And the baby boomer generation rewarded her. As Ed Howker and Shiv Malik note[4]:

> "In 1979 Margaret Thatcher received a 16 percent swing in support from young people aged 18-35 – the baby boomers – significantly more than any other group… Without their support she wouldn't have gained power."

The revolution that Thatcher unleashed was not, however, the revolution she had hoped for. The new breed of entrepreneurs who were supposed to revitalise Britain's manufacturing base, failed to put in an appearance, even as high interest rates and an end to capital controls sent bankruptcies and unemployment soaring. As William Borders reported at the time[5]:

> "Unemployment stands at nearly 9 percent and is increasing so relentlessly that *The Sunday Times* began publishing a weekly listing, headlined 'Jobless Britain,' of factories that have closed and the number of jobs were lost at each. The number unemployed, now well over two million, increased by 900,000 in 1980.
>
> "Industrial production has been declining more sharply than at any time in years, and the rate of inflation is 15 percent. That is lower than the peak reached last summer but still well above the 10 percent inflation when Mrs. Thatcher took office 21 months ago...
>
> "[Thatcher's supporters] like to point to the one bright spot on the economic horizon: the steadily swelling flow of oil from the North Sea. With current production of 1.7 million barrels a day, exceeding such giants as Indonesia and Kuwait, Britain has become self-sufficient in oil, saving this country billions of dollars in import bills...
>
> "But even that good news has a dark side. The oil production has been a major factor in the appreciation of sterling, which is now trading at a level 50 percent higher than in 1976. Though good for some people in Britain, the strong pound has had a devastating effect on exporters, making their goods more expensive abroad...
>
> "Sir Michael Edwardes, the chairman of BL Ltd., the automobile company that used to be called British Leyland, expressed a widely held view among industrialists when he declared in exasperation that, if the Government could not figure out a way to keep the oil from hurting big business, it should 'leave the bloody stuff in the ground.'"

Thatcher's response was her now infamous "the lady's not for turning" speech at the 1981 Tory Party conference, where she also gave the world the acronym TINA – there is no alternative. Despite this bravado though, the Tories had slumped in the polls. And there was every likelihood that a left-leaning Labour government would be returned at the next election. Two events, however, conspired to save Thatcher's bacon and to propel her to a massive electoral majority in 1983. The first was the Argentinian junta's ill-fated decision to invade the Falkland Islands. Thatcher's decision – against the advice of many of her advisors – to retake the islands (ironically with war ships which had already been earmarked for the scrap heap under an austerity review) created an outburst of patriotism which played in the Tories favour. Less obviously but more important electorally, the decision by four prominent Labour MPs[6] to break away and form a new Social Democratic Party (SDP) caused a big split in the opposition vote. While the SDP failed to break through, by depriving Labour of votes it allowed the Tories to extend their 1979 majority by taking swathes of formerly safe Labour seats.

It was during this second Thatcher administration that the neoliberal revolution took shape. On the industrial front, Thatcher unleashed the assault on the coal mining industry with a view to provoking a strike that the Tories were well prepared for. Nevertheless, the strike, when it came, proved to be the longest, largest, and most bitter in Britain's long industrial history. And while memories of Edward Heath's humiliation at the hands of the National Union of Mineworkers (NUM) in 1972 and 1974 remained fresh in Tory minds, the truth was that the miners were a much-weakened force by the mid-1980s. It wasn't just oil that was arriving on shore from the North Sea fields. Natural gas was arriving in massive quantities too. One result of this had been the construction of gas and oil power plants to diversify from coal. This, together with years of coal stockpiling at, and imports to power stations and steelworks prevented the NUM from forcing the economy to a near standstill as it had done in the early 1970s.

The inevitable defeat of the NUM on 3 March 1985 – nearly a year after the strike began – was a huge psychological blow to a Labour movement which had regarded the NUM as a far stronger force than it had actually become. Trade union membership declined throughout the 1980s, and the Labour opposition began to formally embrace Thatcher's brand of neoliberalism.

It was a neoliberalism unwittingly unleashed on 27 October 1986, with the deregulation of Britain's banking and financial sector. The result was precisely the debt-based rentier economy that Kalecki had cautioned against 43 years earlier. Britain – or at least its financial sector in the City of London – became a money-launderer to the world, using its web of offshore tax havens to convert the money held by dictators, corrupt oligarchs and all shades of wide boys into apparently legitimate investments within the western Eurodollar economy.

Previously heavily-regulated banks were suddenly free to create currency – in the form of "bank credit[7]" – whenever they issued loans. Building societies soon got in on the action, bribing their members to allow them to convert to banks so that they, too, could get a share of the free money. Within a matter of years, small provincial banks like the Midland and the Royal Bank of Scotland were turned into globe-spanning behemoths as a result of the income they were making from the securitised debt they had issued and sold.

As we now know to our cost, the "Big Bang" financial deregulation unleashed a globe-spanning Ponzi scheme which required ever more new borrowers to keep the pyramid growing. So that once the *rate* of borrowing fell between 2006 and 2008, the entire system began to unravel. But that isn't how it looked at the time. In order to sell securities, banks had to issue new debt. And one way or another, the currency borrowed into existence found its way into the real economy. Underpinning it were the oil and gas exports from the North Sea, which allowed UK debt to spiral upward *without* undermining the value of the Pound on international markets. As Ian Jack, reminiscing in an article for the *Guardian* recalled[8]:

> "I had the idea for the title when I was walking through a London square around the time of the City's deregulatory 'Big Bang' and Peregrine Worsthorne coining the phrase 'bourgeois triumphalism' to describe the brash behaviour of the newly enriched: the boys who wore red braces and swore long and loud in restaurants. Champagne was becoming an unexceptional drink. The miners had been beaten. A little terraced house in an ordinary bit of London would buy 7.5 similar houses in Bradford. In the seven years since 1979, jobs in manufacturing had declined from about seven million to around five million, and more than nine in every 10 of all jobs lost were located north of the diagonal between the Bristol channel and the Wash. And yet it was also true that more people owned more things – tumble dryers and deep freezers – than ever before, and that the average household's disposable income in 1985 was more than 10% higher than it had been in the last days of Jim Callaghan's government.
>
> "Social peace had been bought by tax cuts and welfare benefits, and these had been largely enabled by government income from North Sea oil that by the mid-1980s was delivering the Treasury 10% of its revenues. The question was, how long would this bounty last?"

Oil and gas will no doubt continue to be recovered from the North Sea for years to come. But two dates stand out here. The first is 1999 – the year that North Sea production peaked. It would have been sooner but for the collapse in production following the 1988 Piper Alpha disaster. Indeed, a reasonable case can be made[9] that had it not been for Piper Alpha, John Major's government would not have had to face the Black Wednesday crisis in 1992, and with the economy much stronger on the back of oil revenues in the mid-1990s, Major might even have gone on to win the 1997 election.

The second key date is 2005 – the year the UK became a net importer of oil and gas. The exact implications of this have been confused because this is also the year that global *conventional* oil production peaked; sending prices and interest rates upward and beginning the process of unravelling which led to the banking crisis in 2008. Nevertheless, the one thing we can say about the post-2008 UK economy is that – at best – it has flatlined.

This was a very different outcome to the one Thatcher had intended all those years earlier. Her version of a revolution involved a new generation of entrepreneurs investing their wealth in new, leading-edge technologies in a UK economy freed from the dead hand of state bureaucracy. The employment revolution she had envisioned involved a better-educated workforce joining world-leading hi-tech companies in exchange for salaries far higher than anything their parents might have dreamed of. Instead, we ended up with an 80:20 rentier economy in which success for the 20 percent depended on selling access to unproductive income generating assets, while the bottom 80 percent ended up in relatively low-paid routine work mostly in the unproductive administration, retail, and hospitality sectors. So that throughout the late 1990s and early 2000s, homeowners drew a bigger income from their houses than their children could make working in High Street stores, restaurants, and offices.

At a dinner in Bournemouth in 2002, an ageing Margaret Thatcher was asked what she thought her greatest success had been. Her instant reply was "Tony Blair and New Labour... we made our opponents change their minds." There is considerable truth to this. For while many on the political left had hoped that Blair really did have some "third way" that was different to both stifling state socialism and untrammelled economic liberalism, the reality was that Blair's three governments served to consolidate and build upon neoliberalism.

The Blair compromise was that, in exchange for accepting and extending economic liberalism, he would usher-in a new brand of authoritarian social neoliberalism... what is today referred to as "social justice" by its supporters and "woke" by its opponents. It is telling that despite the UK manufacturing sector being three times the size of the banking and financial sector in 1992 when John Major defeated Kinnock's Labour Party, the new Labour leadership triad – John Smith, Tony Blair and Gordon Brown – opted to court the rentiers in the City. As Robin Ramsay notes[10]:

> "The figures who created New Labour, the late John Smith, Tony Blair and Gordon Brown, did not meet with the representatives of the domestic economy: the Confederation of British Industry and chambers of commerce, say. Instead they embarked on a 'prawn cocktail offensive' in the City of London and attended the annual Bilderberg meeting, on whose steering committee John Smith sat from 1989-92 while in the shadow cabinet..."

Far from putting an end to "rip off Britain" as they had promised in their 1997 manifesto, New Labour was already committed to a degree of private sector involvement in the public sphere – including the rip-off Public-Private Initiative schemes – which would have made Thatcher blush. Nor was the New Labour project any more beneficent on the social front. After 18 years of Tory pension and welfare cuts, there was some hope that New Labour would restore the social safety net which had kept an earlier generation out of poverty. It wasn't to be. Indeed, New Labour imported the American system in which insurance-busting corporations were employed to find loopholes to deny social security even to those who clearly qualified for it. Moreover, New Labour's cargo cult solution to poverty was not to put a safety net beneath it, but rather to oblige people to re-train for better paid work which might or might not arrive at some later date.

A genuinely social democratic government might, in 2008, have allowed the banks to go bust and then nationalise their assets, recapitalising them with newly created currency from the Bank of England. Instead, Gordon Brown and his Chancellor Alistair Darling chose to throw the people under the bus in order to follow their American counterparts in bailing out the banks and then re-installing the same people who had caused the problem in the first place. The result was the lost decade between the crash and the arrival of the Covid. This was a period in which the income (adjusted for inflation) of the bottom 50 percent of wage earners in the UK went backward. As Pascale Bourquin and Tom Waters from the *Institute for Fiscal Studies* report[11]:

> "The two key characteristics of the labour market over the period bookended by the Great Recession and the onset of the COVID-19 crisis were the strong employment growth and the weak pay growth. The former was widely shared and was strongest for those demographic groups that started out with low employment rates – including immigrants, lone parents and older workers. **The weak pay growth probably stands out as the worst attribute of the labour market over the period: at the median, hourly pay actually fell slightly**, and though wages grew faster at the bottom of

the distribution, the pace was fairly meagre by historical standards... (My emphasis)

"In terms of living standards and poverty, there were certainly plenty of challenges before the COVID-19 crisis – the weakness in earnings growth and benefit cuts had been putting a lot of pressure on incomes at the bottom. But there is no question that large falls in unemployment, and particularly in household worklessness, had been a significant factor in keeping poverty lower than it would otherwise have been. The current crisis may mean that much of that will be undone, with few countervailing forces to prevent more vulnerable households from falling into hardship..."

By this point, however, employment itself had come to be redefined beyond all practical meaning. In the 1970s, there was a clear distinction between people who had jobs and people who did not – although the Department for Health and Social Security often used to turn a blind eye to unemployed workers engaging in casual seasonal work such as fruit and vegetable picking at harvest time. By 2008, it was entirely possible for someone to be in low-paid full-time employment *and* to qualify for social security in the form of Working Tax Credits (now incorporated into Universal Credit). Employment, in turn, is now defined as working anything more than *one hour* per week. And by "employment," this increasingly means low-paid, part-time, zero-hours and gig working of a kind that requires a top-up from the state to provide a minimal standard of living. By the time the Covid arrived, the oft-repeated belief that "work is the route out of poverty," had been demonstrably disproved by the growth of neoliberalism's precariat class.

The psychological impact of the neoliberal revolution has been even more profound. Although this is not obvious to those who regard trades unions as an irredeemable bad, most of the time they do not engage in the sowing of discontent or the promoting of strikes. The key role that they used to play was, in fact, as a useful feedback mechanism for managers. In a sense, they could – and did – act as an official whistle-blower, bringing problems to the attention of management without the need for those affected to be identified. By cutting away these formal structures and protections, neoliberalism denied managers an essential source of feedback which might prevent them from presiding over disasters of one kind or another later on.

At the same time, workers were themselves under far greater pressure to turn a blind-eye, keep their heads down, and let someone else deal with the consequences of idiocy and malpractice. The process of "crackpot realism," which academics had identified as a problem in the immediate aftermath of the Second World War, has become ubiquitous after four decades of neoliberalism. As John Michael Greer explains[12]:

> "Crackpot realism is one of the downsides of the division of labor. It emerges reliably whenever two conditions are in effect. The first condition is that the task of choosing goals for an activity is assigned to one group of people and the task of finding means to achieve those goals is left to a different group of people. The second condition is that the first group needs to be enough higher in social status than the second group that members of the first group need pay no attention to the concerns of the second group...
>
> "Consider, as an example, the plight of a team of engineers tasked with designing a flying car. People have been trying to do this for more than a century now, and the results are in: it's a really dumb idea... Engineers know this. Still, if you're an engineer and you've been hired by some clueless tech-industry godzillionaire who wants a flying car, you probably don't have the option of

telling your employer the truth about his pet project—that is, that no matter how much of his money he plows into the project, he's going to get a clunker of a vehicle that won't be any good at either of its two incompatible roles—because he'll simply fire you and hire someone who will tell him what he wants to hear."

Doubtless, almost all of us have had the experience of carrying out an idiotic instruction simply because it is easier to do so than to answer back. For the most part these will have been relatively trivial examples of crackpot realism in action. Suppose though, you are the co-pilot of a jet airliner – a role which might bring you into conflict with your far more experienced and esteemed captain. Now suppose that you realise that your captain is about to disregard the instructions from the control tower and attempt to take off in thick fog. That's the situation that the co-pilot of KLM flight 4805 from Tenerife to Amsterdam found himself in on Sunday 27 March 1977. And his turning a blind eye – probably fearing the ramifications of challenging a far more experienced captain – was a key reason for what is still the world's worst aircraft disaster, in which 583 people died when the KLM jet struck a PanAm plane that had not cleared the runway.

While air safety has improved considerably – largely due to computers removing this kind of human error from the process – the in-bred irrational psychological flaws in human beings persist. And neoliberal cutting away of social controls and monetisation of social relationships often conspire to create the conditions for great harm. To the technocrats charged with managing everything from businesses to nation states, our acquiescence – like that of the co-pilot on KLM flight 4805 – has been taken as an endorsement of their rule and a measure of their supreme omnipotence. But they are deluded. Margaret Heffernan presents a litany of examples of high-level CEOs and technocrats presiding over such ills as blowing up oil refineries and polluting the Gulf of Mexico, through poisoning entire mining towns to bringing about the worst economic crash in living memory. In almost every case, *our* acquiescence was taken as approval for *their* actions. But even on the very few occasions when someone spoke out – such as the engineers arguing against launching the ill-fated *Challenger* space shuttle – they were dismissed as cranks and conspiracy theorists.

Of course, every time technocratic wrongdoing comes to public attention, establishment media ramp up demands for inquiries and for governments to regulate and legislate harder. But government itself has been largely hollowed out during four decades of neoliberalism. To both the elected representatives and the permanent administration, neoliberalism promised power without responsibility. To give a popular example of this, consider the introduction of the Minimum Wage. Only a minority argue against the idea that there needs to be some floor underneath pay – although there is plenty of scope for argument about where exactly that floor should be. The key benefit to the political class, however, is that while they enjoy the *power* of setting the rate, it falls to businesses to be *responsible* for putting it into practice.

Historically, in the pre-neoliberal common law system[13], government was more concerned with administration than with legislation. Administration, that is, of the various *critical* infrastructure and services – such as roads, electrical grids, armies, and police forces – that allow a society to operate and prosper. Moreover, prior to World War Two, administration was more often the preserve of local rather than national government. In the course of the neoliberal revolution though, local government became – with a degree of justification – a convenient whipping boy for a fast-centralising legislative state. Just as the state forces employers to pay a minimum wage without providing any additional funding, so local government has been tasked with providing everything from childcare services to buses and schools to pothole-free roads, while only being provided with the funds to achieve a fraction of these. One result has been the loss of a raft of supposedly "non-essential" services like music lessons, school playing fields, libraries and parks, as local councils struggle to fund their statutory duties.

Nevertheless, among neoliberalism's many big lies was the one about "rolling back the state." Despite the rhetoric, the central state continued growing throughout the Thatcher, Major and Blair years, so that the state is bigger – in both cost and numbers employed – today than ever before[14]. And yet, at the same time, the critical infrastructure and services that the state directly provides is far smaller than it was in the 1980s thanks to various privatisations and public-private partnerships. This is reflected to a large degree in the educational and employment backgrounds of the political class.

Prior to the 2019 general election – when a new intake of "red wall Tories" began to alter the cosy occupational balance – the number of MPs with *real* work experience – either running or working in a business – had been in steep decline. When New Labour arrived in government, the majority of MPs were lawyers, which, perhaps, explains why they were so keen on passing volumes of new legislation but not sure about how to enforce it all. Not that the rot stopped with lawyers. By the time David Cameron and George Osborne took over, the majority of MPs were Philosophy, Politics and Economics graduates who had previously interned and then worked as special advisors to other politicians. Internships, of course, limit accessibility to those with rich enough parents to support them while they work for free. And the special advisor route to office – either as an elected member or as a new breed of civil servant – meant that by the 2010s, the political class had become a self-perpetuating technocracy too.

The irony is that just at the point when the political class – and, indeed, the technocracy as a whole – was emerging as a "class for itself," the 2008 financial crash and the ensuing depression changed the rules of the game. Most of us, it turns out, were content to turn a blind-eye to the raft of corporate and governmental wrongdoing that neoliberalism creates *so long as* our living standards were growing. In this respect, the neoliberal settlement was similar to the unwritten pact between the Chinese Communist Party and the Chinese people – trading political extremism for economic prosperity. In the wake of the crash though, median wages have been falling steadily, and less visibly prosperity – life beyond essentials like housing, heating, food and clean water – has fallen sharply (reflected at the bottom of the income ladder by the massive growth of in-work poverty and foodbank use).

From a purely theoretical standpoint, many anticipated that the parties of the political left would grow in strength as people faced declining living standards resulting from deliberate government austerity policies such as the imposition of the "bedroom tax" and the underfunding of the new Universal Credit system. The neoliberal, New Labour revolution, however, had changed the Labour Party and the labour movement forever. Although wedded to a *hypothetical* support for the working class, the left had failed to notice the huge shift in the class structure which had occurred during four decades of neoliberalism.

Two differences were crucial to understanding the backlash which began in 2016. First, and most obviously, the massed ranks of disciplined and organised industrial labour had all but disappeared – the factories shipped off to China, South Korea and Vietnam, and the mines, steelworks and shipyards pared down to a bare strategic minimum. In their place a massive new precariat class – having little control of their lives and pinballed in and out of low paid gig, zero-hours and part-time working – had grown across

1970s Inequality

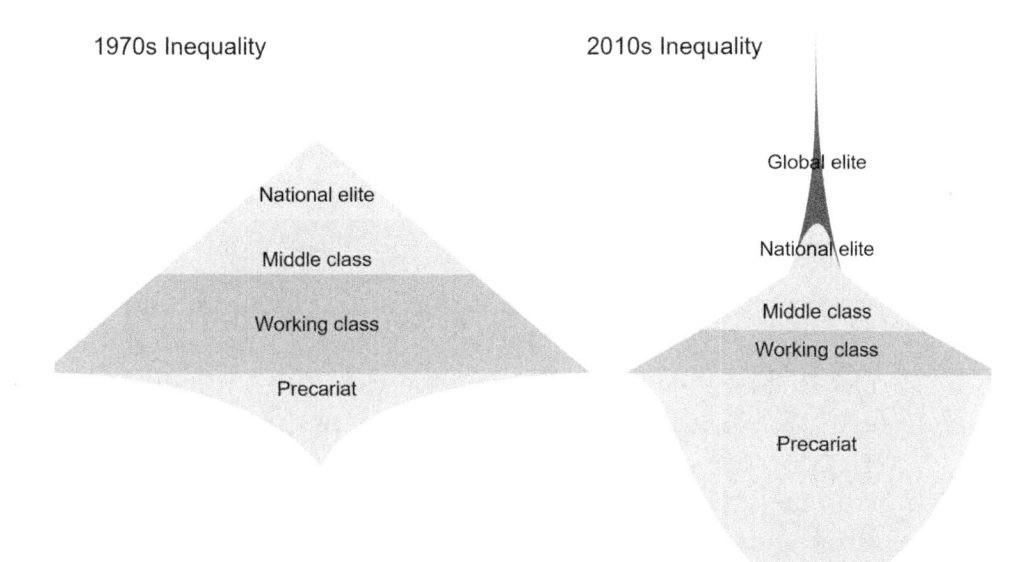

- National elite
- Middle class
- Working class
- Precariat

2010s Inequality

- Global elite
- National elite
- Middle class
- Working class
- Precariat

ex-industrial, rundown seaside and small-town Britain. Insofar as some skilled industrial workers remain, these are more akin to what the left used to call "the aristocracy of labour" – a relatively privileged sub-class whose high pay and good working conditions tend to result in a neoliberal political and economic outlook.

The second, and less obvious change has been the development of a single global elite to replace and eclipse the national elites which once ruled individual nation states. These are people who move effortlessly between global cities like New York, Tokyo, Paris and London. They stay in hotels and eat in restaurants that are identical in all of the global cities. And while they reside within each of these cities they go about doing *global* business. A rarely noticed consequence of the rise of this globalist class has been the disconnection of big business from national conservative parties. For example, writing about Britain during the Brexit crisis in the autumn of 2019, historian David Edgerton[15] observed that:

"What is interesting is not so much the connections between capital and the Tory party but their increasing disconnection. Today much of the capital in Britain is not British and not linked to the Conservative party – where for most of the 20th century things looked very different…

"Today there is no such thing as British national capitalism. London is a place where world capitalism does business – no longer one where British capitalism does the world's business. Everywhere in the UK there are foreign-owned enterprises, many of them nationalised industries, building nuclear reactors and running train services from overseas. When the car industry speaks, it is not as British industry but as foreign enterprise in the UK. The same is true of many of the major manufacturing sectors – from civil aircraft to electrical engineering – and of infrastructure. Whatever the interests of foreign capital, they are not expressed through a national political party."

During the neoliberal turn, parties of both centre-left and centre-right had to become more "globalist" in outlook in order to continue to secure the campaign funds they need to fight elections. But one consequence of this has been a growing gulf between the parties and the people. Across Europe, where proportional representation systems allow people to vote for the parties they like most – rather than the ones they dislike least – the old Christian Democrat and Social Democrat parties have all but disappeared (save for Germany where, until recently they were in a coalition together). In Britain, the first-past-the-post voting system continues to benefit the old parties (for now) resulting in division *within* rather than between parties. The rise of the Corbyn left within the Labour Party and the anti-European Union right within the Tory Party mirroring the Sanders wing of the US Democrat Party and the Trump wing of the Republicans.

Like concrete cancer slowly disintegrating the inner core of a concrete and steel building, the changes which neoliberalism had wrought upon the economies of the west had corrupted the very foundations of the system itself. What had begun as an attempt to undermine the power of organised labour went on to corrode the power of governments, businesses, and national elites in their turn. Only faceless global banks and corporations and the deranged technocrats they employ remained to lord it over the minions who had been conned into handing power to them. But so rotten was the economic structure that they presided over that it would only take an unforeseen shock to begin the collapse of the entire edifice.

That shock came in two connected parts in the first decade of the twenty-first century. First, and seldom commented upon, came the peak of global *conventional* (i.e., cheap and easy) oil production – sending prices spiralling upward across the economy and upsetting the delicate balance between debt and growth. Second, and partly a consequence of the oil shock, the unravelling of bad debt across the western economies resulted in bank runs and bankruptcies which were only halted via state bailouts, quantitative easing and near zero percent interest rates – all of which halted the collapse but *did nothing* to restore the system to health.

Since 2008, the majority of the population of the western economies has seen its living standards decline. Some form of political backlash was inevitable. Indeed, in the wake of the crash, some even anticipated a twenty-first century version of the Leninist coup of October 1917. When it arrived though, the uprising proved to be very different to anything anyone could imagine.

Notes

1. Kalecki, M. 1943. "Political Aspects of Full Employment." *Political Quarterly*.

2. In their day, "inflation" referred only to price increases *resulting from* an expansion of currency, and excluded, for example, price increases resulting from supply-side shocks such as food or energy shortages. Today, "inflation" is taken to be synonymous with price increases. Thus, using today's definition, inflation *is not* "everywhere and always a monetary phenomenon."

3. Thain, C. and Wright, M. (1995) *The Treasury and Whitehall: The Planning and Control of Public Expenditure, 1976-1993*, London, Clarendon Press.

4. Howker, E. and Malik, S. 2010. *Jilted Generation: How Britain Has Bankrupted Its Youth*. Icon Books

5. "Can Thatcherism Survive British Slump?" *New York Times*. 8 February 1981.

6. Shirley Williams, David Owen, William Rogers and Roy Jenkins.

7. These are the numbers that appear on your and my bank statement, and which allow for electronic transfers of all kinds. They are entirely divorced from cash.

8. "North Sea oil fuelled the 80s boom, but it was, and remains, strangely invisible." *Guardian*. 19 April 2013.

9. I make the case in "The disaster that led to New Labour." *Consciousness of Sheep*. 25 August 2020. https://consciousnessofsheep.co.uk/2020/08/25/the-disaster-that-led-to-new-labour

10. Ramsay, R. (2012) 'How Labour Embraced the City', *New Left Project*, December 15, 201

11. "Jobs and job quality between the eve of the Great Recession and the eve of COVID-19." 28 July 2021. *Fiscal Studies: Volume 43, Issue 1*

12. *The Terror of Deep Time* - https://www.ecosophia.net/terror-deep-time

13. Broadly, in the common law system everything is permitted unless there is a law preventing it. In the European – Napoleonic – system in contrast, everything is prevented unless there is a law permitting it.

14. "They promised a small state. They gave us a weak state." *Consciousness of Sheep*. https://consciousnessofsheep.co.uk/2017/07/11/they-promised-a-small-state-they-gave-us-a-weak-state

15. Edgerton, D. 9 October 2019. "Brexit is a necessary crisis – it reveals Britain's true place in the world." *Guardian*. https://www.theguardian.com/commentisfree/2019/oct/09/brexit-crisis-global-capitalism-britain-place-world

Just make it stop

Peculiar to the present moment is the manner in which both "left" and "right" appear to reject the neoliberal order. Conservatives look on in horror at the financialisation and individualisation of traditional structures of family, community, and nation, even as a fake left complains about institutional inequalities and the destruction wrought on the ecosystems we depend upon. Even the "silent majority" is lurching from one political extreme to its opposite and back again in search of someone or something which will return some stability to their increasingly precarious lives. Only the technocracy seems content with a situation in which nations and economies have been hollowed out in service of some imagined globalist utopia. Despite this widespread discontent with the established order though, no alternative has emerged. As Martin Gurri laments, in the age of social media[1]:

> "The public rides on new technologies and platforms, but as users rather than makers: it is uninterested in leveraging technical innovation to formulate its own ideology, programs, or plans. The public opposes, but does not propose. So in the second decade of the new millennium, political arguments resemble a distorted echo of the French Revolution or Victorian England: we still quarrel in terms of left and right, conservative and liberal, even while the old landscape has been swept clean and the relevance of these venerable labels has become uncertain. The lack of new alternatives, of a way out, has trapped democratic politics in a perpetual feedback loop of failure and negation. And negation, invoked from every corner and without relief, has driven the democratic process to the edge of nihilism—the belief that the status quo is so abhorrent that destruction will be a form of progress."

Conservatives, whose historic role was to defend traditional structures and values lest we inadvertently cut down the very foundations of our way of life, fell asleep at the wheel sometime in the 1980s, when the neoliberal trojan horse arrived draped in the disguise of a new conservatism. For all of the conservative rhetoric, the revolution ushered in by Thatcher, Reagan and Mitterrand was neoliberal to its uncaring corporatist core. And far from rejuvenating the tired national economies of the 1970s, it willingly vandalised the industrial and agricultural base, while handing the keys to the kingdom to a global banking and financial monster which owed neither fealty nor obligation to any nation or people. Only now, as conservatives find themselves on the losing side of a corporate-inspired culture war, have they woken up to the damage done to ordinary families and communities across the western world... damage which they more than most might have done something to prevent had they not turned a blind eye to it when their chosen team was in government.

The fake left is no less impotent, having mindlessly sold its soul to a global corporate technocracy which openly refers to its supporters as useful idiots. As Paul Kingsnorth recently observed[2]:

> "Progressive leftism and global capitalism, far from being antagonistic as some of us once thought, have turned out to be a usefully snug fit. Both are totalising, utopian projects. Both are suspicious of the past, impatient with borders and boundaries, and hostile to religion, superstition and the limits on the human individual imposed by nature or culture...

> "Despite much self-mythologising, leftist ideology has always been primarily a product of urban intellectuals and middle-class radicals pursuing a project of theoretical levelling. This levelling always begins with the destruction of previous lifeways — Mao's four olds, the

Bolshevik project to eliminate the 'bourgeois family' (currently being resurrected by some on the contemporary Left), French revolutionary attempts to rationalise the landscape, the current progressive push to "transition" children — but what it ends up doing is clearing the ground for the Machine."

Spot the difference

Old Left	Fake Left
Class solidarity	Fragmentation by identity group
Anti-capitalist	Pro "stakeholder" capitalism
Democratic	Corporatist
Anti-imperialist	Pro-western imperialism
Anti-war	Pro-war
Against secret police	Pro-secret police
Pro-free speech	Pro-censorship
Controlled immigration	Open borders
Materialist	Idealist
Reason	Emotion
Pro-science	Anti-science
Social democracy	Social neoliberal
Pro-human	Anti-human

One glaringly obvious – to anyone who cares to notice – consequence of this is the way in which neoliberal state authorities embrace fake left protest. No longer do we witness mounted police stampeding over women and children as occurred in Whitehall during the 1990 Poll Tax demonstration. Gone is the age-old sound of a police batten cracking the skull of a picketing trade unionist. Only when the wrong kind of protestors – such as those who opposed the 2020-21 lockdowns and vaccine passports – take to the streets do the police dust down their paramilitary riot gear.

But when the fake left rallies for Black Lives Matter, trans rights, women's safety or the Green New deal, the police don flat caps and shirt sleeves, and regularly join in with the carnival atmosphere.

The point being that, if any of these fake left protests were in any way threatening to the technocracy and the global elite, the riot sticks and water cannons would be brought out and the protestors subjected to a degree of violence last seen in response to the London riots in 2011, which, despite beginning in response to the police shooting of Mark Duggan, were entirely apolitical and aimed largely at liberating consumer durables like phones, TVs and trainers from the corporate shops along Oxford Street, As Gurri recalls[3]:

> "There were no Facebook invitations to the London riots, as there had been to Tahrir Square and Puerta del Sol. But there was active use by the participants of BlackBerry Messaging Service, or BMS, a private texting channel favored by the young in the affected communities. The Economist christened the disturbances 'The BlackBerry Riots.' The global information sphere was at work in London in August 2011. Also unlike the other events of 2011, criminal behavior was the salient feature of the riots. Many of those arrested had experienced previous brushes with the law, and one in four had committed more than 10 past offenses..."

If you can't win within the system and there is no obvious way of changing it, then helping yourself to those of its products that you couldn't otherwise afford proves to be more rational than, say, gluing yourself to a painting in the expectation that this might result in the technocracy ending fossil fuel use. This, too, points to an essential feature of neoliberalism... it is not amenable to change.

This may not be immediately obvious since the whole point of neoliberalism is *permanent* change. But in this respect, it is like a supertanker moving on a steady course from which it will not be diverted. That course began with the financialisation of every aspect of our way of life, even as the system itself has metastasised in an attempt to impose its order upon every nation and every person on the planet. It is fundamentally anti-democratic, handing the reins of power to unelected technocrats from the "correct" schools and universities, to manage those branches of state and corporations over which they claim a technical expertise. It is also authoritarian since the people are always and everywhere an implicit – and occasionally overt – threat to technocracy. And, of course, it is iconoclastic, torching every custom and structure which stands in the way of its pursuit of its one-world digital utopia.

Environmental issues are central to the current iteration of neoliberal technocracy but remain secondary to the primary aim of financialising, assimilating, and digitising every aspect of human life on planet Earth. That is, while it is true that three centuries of an expanding industrial economy has damaged Earth's ecosystems to the point that human life support systems are threatened, the neoliberal technocracy demands only those "solutions" which fit *within* its primary aims. Thus, for example, when Margaret Thatcher addressed the United Nations on 8 November 1989[4], she had no hesitation in placing the environment front and centre of the neoliberal stage:

> "Of all the challenges faced by the world community in those four years, one has grown clearer than any other in both urgency and importance—I refer to the threat to our global environment...
>
> "What we are now doing to the world, by degrading the land surfaces, by polluting the waters and by adding greenhouse gases to the air at an unprecedented rate—all this is new in the experience of the earth. It is mankind and his activities which are changing the

environment of our planet in damaging and dangerous ways...

"We are seeing a vast increase in the amount of carbon dioxide reaching the atmosphere. The annual increase is three billion tonnes: and half the carbon emitted since the Industrial Revolution still remains in the atmosphere.

"At the same time as this is happening, we are seeing the destruction on a vast scale of tropical forests which are uniquely able to remove carbon dioxide from the air..."

The same words could just as easily slip off the tongue of Greta Thunberg or any one of today's Extinction Rebellion campaigners. But this is to miss the primary purpose of the speech, which was to promote a neoliberal response to the changing climate as the *only* option:

"It is no good squabbling over who is responsible or who should pay. Whole areas of our planet could be subject to drought and starvation if the pattern of rains and monsoons were to change as a result of the destruction of forests and the accumulation of greenhouse gases.

"We have to look forward not backward and we shall only succeed in dealing with the problems through a vast international, co-operative effort...

"**But as well as the science, we need to get the economics right**. That means first **we must have continued economic growth** in order to generate the wealth required to pay for the protection of the environment. But it must be growth which does not plunder the planet today and leave our children to deal with the consequences tomorrow.

"And second, **we must resist the simplistic tendency to blame modern multinational industry** for the damage which is being done to the environment. Far from being the villains, it is on them that we rely to do the research and find the solutions.

"It is industry which will develop safe alternative chemicals for refrigerators and air-conditioning. It is industry which will devise bio-degradable plastics. It is industry which will find the means to treat pollutants and make nuclear waste safe—and many companies as you know already have massive research programmes…" (My emphasis)

The response to climate change, then, must be led by global corporations operating within a corporatist version of a "free market" in which economic growth is essential. Here, of course, many environmental campaigners would push back – although never to the point of rejecting the neoliberal technocracy's "bright green" version of combatting climate change – pointing out that it is *growth* which created the problem in the first place. Population, wealth, and pollution have risen in lockstep with and are a product of the rise in energy – primarily from fossil fuels – consumed in the economy. For many campaigners, the myth of "green growth" central to such projects as "net zero," "the fourth industrial revolution," "the green new deal," and "the great reset" are little more than a veneer of greenwash covering the same old capitalistic imperialism.

The result of Thatcher's version of green neoliberal technocracy is seen in Jeff Gibb's film *Planet of the Humans*[4], in which global corporations and bought off campaigners are exposed for greenwashing environmentally destructive activities in pursuit of profit. A more detailed critique of the myth of green growth can be found in *Bright Green Lies*[5], where Derrick Jensen, Lierre Keith and Max Wilbert systematically debunk the technologies that are central to the neoliberal technocratic environmental response. Wind, solar and other modern energy technologies are *not* renewable even if the energy source is for all practical purposes. None of these technologies can be constructed, transported, deployed, and maintained without the use of fossil fuels at every stage. In practice, they are non-renewable renewable energy-harvesting technologies (NRREHTs) and, crucially, they are a – albeit highly lucrative – blind alley for addressing our environmental problems.

Notably, both *Planet of the Humans* and *Bright Green Lies* were met with vitriol from those supposedly left-leaning and environmentally aware media outlets which not that long ago would have devoted pages of content to exposing capitalist corporations cashing in on our environmental concerns. Moreover, the attack on both was ad hominem – accusing the authors of being "climate deniers" – rather than a grounded response challenging the evidence. As with "woke" more generally, anyone who criticises the neoliberal technocratic corporate approach to the perceived problem must be shouted down, censored, cancelled lest their rational scepticism break the propagandist spell.

In this way, the mass of protestors who might otherwise oppose the corporate-owned, neoliberal version of "green growth" are co-opted into support for an agenda which is against their own interests. Meanwhile, alternative responses to environmental overshoot, such as managed de-growth are unable to break through to public consciousness while the fake left act as useful idiots on behalf of the technocracy.

This points to an erosion of protest as profound as neoliberalism's impact on the wider economy and society. While focussing primarily on the impact of social media, Gurri demonstrates the ultimate impotence of the wave of "occupy"-type protest which erupted following the 2008 crash and the 2011 Arab Spring. These were truly massive demonstrations, but with the exception of Tunisia and a brief democratic interregnum in Egypt, nothing changed.

The same neoliberal governments were re-elected and the technocracy continued its work unimpeded.

The glaringly obvious reason for this is that sit-ins and protest marches don't change anything. None of the bankers were held to account in the wake of the occupy protests. And the financial alchemy which allows banks to create debt-based currency out of thin air, and then create a mountain of derivatives based upon it, has continued apace. For all of the noise and nuisance generated by climate activists in groups like Extinction Rebellion, Insulate Britain and Just Stop Oil, fossil fuel consumption and carbon emissions continued to rise unabated until November 2018, when global oil production peaked. And it has taken a war in Ukraine to force European governments to make the cuts to fossil fuel consumption that they have been promising for decades. The Black Lives Matter protests did not prevent a single black person from being gunned down in the street. Indeed, in one of life's tragic ironies, the leader of BLM in the UK, Sasha Johnson became the victim of a "black on black" drive-by shooting in May 2021, where she received "catastrophic and permanent injuries."

As Anthony Stafford Beer once pointed out, "the purpose of a system is what it does," since we wouldn't spend all of that time and energy failing to do something else. It is hard, therefore, not to conclude that the primary reason for the persistence of protest of this kind is creating and strengthening tribal bonds... virtue signalling being the secondary purpose – since bringing about substantial change is something that has occurred so infrequently that it was hardly worth the bother.

A key reason for this is simply that neoliberalism didn't end with the erosion of the trade unions, like rust it continued to eat its way through *all* of our institutions. The same economic vandalism which saw millions of productive workers cast onto the dole queue, resulted in the offshoring of industry to the point that we no longer had "British industry" but rather the UK branches of global industry. German and Spanish corporations run our trains, Chinese and French corporations run our power stations, Indian corporations run our steelworks and Japanese corporations operate our car assembly plants. And all of them depend upon complex supply chains to produce and deliver the component parts without which the system will collapse.

In this environment, politicians themselves become technocratic specialists. Specialists, that is, in getting elected. And the tried and tested means of achieving this end has been to tack to the imagined "centre ground." This, in turn, pits elected politicians against their – usually more radical – party members. Indeed, the British Labour Party has developed something of a fetish for periodically expelling its more radical members. The result though, is that traditional means of swaying party policy have all but disappeared. For example, in the 1970s the conferences of the Confederation of British Industry and the Trades Union Congress were forces to be reckoned with because policies developed there would often become party policy going into the next general election.

External – "third sector" – organisations have also, on occasion, been able to influence public policy. During the mid-1990s, for example, when Blair's New Labour were in opposition, they used friendly charities, non-profits, and quangos as a kind of shadow civil service, carrying out the research needed to inform the policies in the highly successful 1997 manifesto. The quid pro quo was that the state provided grants and contracts to the same organisations to guarantee their funding. The not unreasonable criticism of this arrangement was that New Labour had created a large number of "sock puppet" organisations which only *appeared* to be independent of government. The result was that while *some* opposition was possible, these state-funded bodies would always bend to the will of the government if their funding was at risk.

Critical to this arrangement was an old post-war division between charities *for* various interest groups as opposed to charities *of* those groups. Many of today's giant charities – Mind, Mencap, the Royal Institute for the deaf, etc. – began life as a series of "councils for," set up, funded and their members appointed by the post-war labour government. And while their modern iterations "consult" and "involve" their respective victim groups, their boards of directors continue to be made up of "the great and the good." The tone and type of policy which emanates from these bought and paid for groups is very different to the tone and approach of far less popular groups run by and for those with particular needs, such as Disabled People Against Cuts. These groups generally eschew and resent the victim status imposed upon them by mainstream charities, arguing instead that it is state policy rather than personal characteristics which disables people. But since these views fall outside the "Overton window" of acceptable (neoliberal) argument, they are seldom covered by the establishment media and barely ever sway politicians.

To add to the problem, campaign groups of this kind have been subjected to regulation and legislation designed to mute criticism of the government. The bigger, state-friendly charities are better able to deal with the additional bureaucracy because they can afford to employ administrators and managers, and to pay for legal advice. Small, user-led organisations, in contrast, are easily shut out of political discourse despite being far better placed to represent their members' views. And so, once again, an older means of participating in the political process – the campaign group – is rendered impotent under a neoliberal technocracy.

The same is true of the age-old practice of petitioning. There had been a time when a large petition would carry considerable weight with politicians. It takes tenacity to go door-to-door in all weathers gathering thousands of signatures. But in the internet age, it is possible to obtain hundreds of thousands of electronic petition signatures at the click of a button. And politicians have altered their views accordingly. For example, in the wake of the Brexit referendum, the UK Parliament website received more than a million signatures on a petition in favour of a second referendum. But the then Leader of the House dismissed the petition, stating that the government would take notice when it received 17.5 million signatures (the number of people who voted to leave the EU). Petitioning government may be easier now than ever before but getting government to take notice is all the harder.

It is hard not to conclude that there is no longer a *peaceful* means for the public to influence the state. Protest has been usurped by corporate interests; political parties present only a lesser of two evils choice for the electorate – guaranteeing that evil always wins. Campaigning and petitioning are rendered largely ineffective by state funding of sock-puppets and by the use of law and regulation to neuter those which might challenge the neoliberal order. And so, we have the irony that, at a time when social media makes it easier than ever to witness the corruption, lies and errors of the technocracy, and at a time when a majority of people from across the political spectrum are unhappy with the status quo, our collective ability to bring about change is weaker than ever.

Notes

1. Gurri, M. The Revolt of The Public and the Crisis of Authority in the New Millennium (p. 271). Stripe Press. Kindle Edition

2. Kingsnorth, P. 5 July 2022. "How the Left fell for capitalism." *UnHerd*. https://unherd.com/2022/07/how-the-left-fell-for-capitalism

3. Gurri, M. The Revolt of The Public and the Crisis of Authority in the New Millennium (p. 153). Stripe Press. Kindle Edition

4. Speech to United Nations General Assembly (Global Environment). Thatcher Archive. https://www.margaretthatcher.org/document/107817

5. https://planetofthehumans.com

6. Jensen, D., Keith, L and Wilbert, M. 2021. *Bright Green Lies: How the environmental movement lost its way and what we can do about it.* Monkfish Book Publishing

There's more to this picture

Modern society may seldom have been as divided as it is today. Tribal factions have emerged over all and every issue – trans versus feminists, MAGA versus BLM and antifa, climate activists versus climate denialists, brexiteers versus remainiacs, etc... once an issue rises to prominence, it is only a matter of time before sides are taken and tribal factions emerge. Social media algorithms work to push people to the extremes, widening and intensifying the divide. At which point any hope of a rational debate is lost as group identity takes priority... we don't have to be right; we just have to signal our conservative outrage or our woke piety. For all of the noise and animosity on either side of this schism, I want to suggest that if we drill down deep enough, we will find an essential common ground among all of these warring tribes. Because the core evil that each seeks to overcome is a quasi-religious state of bereavement that we might call "progress lost."

Progress – the ever upward arc of human knowledge, human ingenuity and of human living standards – is the closest thing that the mass of the western population has to a religion following the death of God in the long nineteenth century. At the beginning of that period, the Earth was a mere six thousand years old. And all of the animals and plants over which God had granted humanity stewardship, were exactly as they had been when the Earth was created. A little over half a century later, those certainties had gone. Geologists had demonstrated that planet Earth was more than four *billion* years old. Darwin and Wallace had unveiled a process of evolution which could only occur over millions of years. And a few chemists were coming around to the idea that the coal which was powering an industrial revolution might actually be fossilised plants heated and crushed within the Earth's crust over millions of years. The final blow was struck in the hot summer of 1914, when, "with God at their side," the massed armies of five European empires embarked on four years of slaughter for a cause that no general, priest nor Emperor could explain.

When it was all over, the only certainty left for we mere mortals to cling to in the hope that life is something more than a random accident, was the *technological* progress which could (in the developed states) be seen all around us. As biologist Steve Jones argues, the bicycle – the first form of affordable mass transport and one of the most energy-efficient – allowed for a massive revolution in the human genome as men and women could travel – and meet potential partners – beyond their hometowns for the first time. The development of railways and their accessibility to ordinary people pushed geographical and social mobility further forward. The giant, steam-powered ocean liners of the late nineteenth and early twentieth century paved the way for regular intercontinental travel and migration – including the wave of indentured mass migration which provided the labour force for American industrialisation. During the war, aeroplanes had developed from flimsy contraptions held together with glue and paper to sturdy fighters and bombers, setting the stage for the peacetime development of air transport in the inter-war years... people – at least the wealthy ones – no longer needed to imagine what it might be like to fly like a bird – they could board a plane and find out for themselves. Less than half a century later, the science fiction writers' dream of reaching out beyond the confines of planet Earth was made real when the first Americans set foot on the Moon.

For a large part of human existence, people had thought of life in terms of cycles. The calendar year was likely devised to mark the changing seasons, ushering in the spring planting season, the summer growing season and the autumn harvest season, followed by the long, dark winter. The lifecycle was well understood too – lifeforms are born, grow to maturity, begin to atrophy, decline and eventually die. Civilisations too – whether Egyptian, Greek, or Roman – were understood to follow a similar cycle of growth, maturity, decline, and collapse... often at the hands of one or more of the Biblical four horsemen.

Progress, insofar as it appeared at all to preindustrial people, was merely the upward slope of the spiral of growth, maturity, collapse, and death. Only a fool would believe that such an upward slope could continue indefinitely. Beginning, however, with the European enlightenment, people began to imagine the upward arc of progress. Economists like Adam Smith and Anne Robert Jacques Turgot introduced the idea of a permanent upward slope of human development and betterment facilitated by free trade. This, in turn, paved the way for the emergence of two of the three ideologies of progress – liberalism and conservatism.

In his book *Unthinking Social Science*, Immanuel Wallerstein explains the emergence of the three core ideologies of industrial civilisation – Liberalism, Conservatism and Marxism. Despite huge scope for disagreement between them, Wallerstein makes the case that each is a response to a shared belief in *progress*. That is, Liberals – rooted in the emerging industrialist class – view progress as a benign good. And so, liberalism embraces the process of reform which overthrows the old feudal order and ushers in an age of growing material wealth which improves the lot of all. Conservatism emerges as a counterweight to liberal excess. In effect warning against throwing the baby out with the bathwater. Conservatives also believe in the upward slope of progress but warn against pushing it too far and too fast. Structures which provided the foundation for industrial progress in the first place – family, church, nation, etc. – may be seriously undermined to the detriment of all if liberal reforms are allowed to continue unchecked. Peel's formula of "minor reforms for proven abuses," is seen as the best way of managing progress.

Philosophers such as Malthus and de Tocqueville had argued that if there is an upward slope of progress, it is one which undulates through booms and slumps and is punctuated by bitter revolution and war. Using the Hegelian dialectic, Marx attempts to unify the optimism of Smith with the pessimism of Malthus and draws upon the emerging theory of evolution to do so. By the mid-nineteenth century, Marx and his collaborator Engels could write at length about the way in which the industrial working class had been alienated and immiserated. Nevertheless, Marx still argued that the process of industrialisation had enabled humanity to *progress* far beyond the limits imposed by feudalism. The problem as Marx saw it, was not with progress itself, but with the way in which the self-interest of the new bourgeois ruling class acted as a block on further progress. Only by a revolution in which the working class overthrew the industrial ruling class, Marx argued, could a further round of progress begin.

The various criticisms of all three ideologies have been rehearsed many times. The most notable criticism being that each fails in practice. That is, hard material reality is a barrier that can never be transcended with ideas and beliefs alone. And arguably, the most stable political periods have occurred when a pragmatic consensus is arrived at when we agree to *progress* within the material limits which we are presented with. More important for us today is that sometime in the late-1960s and early-1970s we experienced a jarring brake on progress. Working people's living standards, which had been rising across the developed world since the end of World War Two came to an abrupt halt in the early-1970s before rising one last time until 1979, then falling away even as corporate profits began to soar. In the course of the 1980s, what began as a positive – creating equal opportunities for women in the workplace – morphed into a necessity, as home ownership increasingly required two incomes. Over the same period, the things which had made Britain great – old industries like mining, railways, steel working and shipbuilding, together with new industries like aviation and automobiles – had been closed, sold off or offshored, and replaced with less valuable work in services, retail, and hospitality. Only those in the technocracy were still able to afford the suburban middle-class lifestyle... a process which would be repeated to some extent in the USA and much of Europe.

On the bright side, people's living standards were somehow still growing – albeit at a much slower rate and easily eclipsed by the concentration of wealth at the top. But in the debt-fuelled 1990s, aided by the computer and telecommunications sector – the final sector of the economy where some technological development was still happening – it was possible to pretend that progress was still real.

That all came to an end with the financial calamity of 2008, which exposed the shaky foundations on which the western way of life had come to rest. And in the depression which has followed, most people's living standards have declined. Nor does anyone appear to have an alternative to this decline. At the end of 2019, the western economies began to tip into another recession which threatened to expose the ongoing failures in the banking and financial sector. They were saved, however, by the appearance of a relatively mild – and likely lab-manipulated – coronavirus which provided the pretext for governments around the world to lock up their populations and shut down large parts of their economies. The damage that this wreaked is only now being realised in the form of commodity shortages, price volatility, broken supply chains, over-loaded public services, and distorted behaviour in the financial system.

Over the course of this fifty-year downturn, we have witnessed a re-working of the three core ideologies of progress. Following the failed revolutions of 1968, the intellectual, metropolitan thwarted bourgeoise class began to re-write Marxism to by-pass a proletariat which had failed to meet the historical mission Marx had imposed upon it. In place of the old, industrial Marxism, a new Gramscian update of Marxism would attempt to bring about revolution by taking over the cultural heights of society – education, the arts, television, music, etc. Soon after, a militant neo-conservatism began to reassert older, pre-war economic theories as the best means of combatting inflation and restoring growth rates which had demonstrably fallen by the mid-1970s. These provided the foundation for a neoliberal economic policy under Reagan, Thatcher, and Mitterrand in the early-1980s.

The moment of solidification came, eventually, with the election of Bill Clinton in the USA and Tony Blair in the UK. Prior to the accession of these *neoliberal* leaders, the opposition parties had engaged in internal struggles over whether to embrace or repeal the laissez faire market economics of the neo-cons. The Clinton/Blair compromise, which ushered in a new consensus uniting the parties of the neoliberal-left and neoliberal-right, was to trade acceptance of liberal free-market economics in exchange for acceptance of state-imposed social liberalism. It was this compromise which resulted in the technocratic managerial class completing their transition from Marxian revolutionaries to the reactionary defenders of a technocratic neoliberal order, melding corporate and state power, within which they had become entrenched in the cultural heights. And this is one reason that today's self-identifying left despises what remains of the working class whenever it acts in a manner that reminds them – as it did in 2016 – that the massed ranks of ordinary people can still be a force for change. For today's fake left activists, populism – once a defining characteristic of the left – is no longer a force to be embraced and focussed, but an evil to be resisted and exorcised lest it bring down the cosy neoliberal order.

This ideological stalemate gives a clue as to why the various protest movements of the post-2008 period have failed to bring about meaningful change. In the end, the three core ideologies of progress have become incorporated into the neoliberal order in a way which obliges them to defend the technocracy. And so, it is only the ruling elite – through organisations like the European Commission, the World Economic Forum, the IMF and the World Bank – which can set the direction of change, even though such organisations are now so out of touch with ordinary lives and so untethered from material reality that they can only bring about ruin.

Why though, should this have happened just now?

The obvious reason is that the ideologies of progress no longer work. As Mary Harrington pondered during a conversation with philanthropist Peter Thiel[1]:

> "Post-liberal thinkers such as Patrick Deneen, author of the bestselling 2018 book *Why Liberalism Failed*, argue that many contemporary social ills are an effect of the way the liberal project cannibalises social goods, such as family life or religious faith, in order to pursue narrow metrics such as (on the Left) personal freedom or (on the Right) economic growth. Thiel sees many of the same ills as Deneen, but offers a strikingly different framing: we're consuming ourselves not because the fixation on progress is inevitably self-destructive beyond a certain threshold, but because material progress has objectively stalled while we remain collectively in denial about this fact...
>
> "Thiel characterises this stagnation as a long, slow victory of the Club of Rome, a nonprofit founded in 1968 to drive political change premised on the belief that infinite growth is impossible. As Thiel sees it, this tacit postwar abandonment of the growth aspiration has resulted in 'something like a societal and cultural lockdown; not just the last two years but in many ways the last 40 or 50'. There's 'a cultural version, a demographic version, and

a technological version of this stagnant or decadent society,' he suggests. And the upshot of this paralysis has been 'a world of technological stagnation and demographic collapse', along with 'sclerosis in government and banal repetition in culture.'"

Certainly, Thiel's list of symptoms provides a reasonable description of today's impotent malaise. The American Dream of the post-war years, in which we could unite around the idea that each new generation should be better off than the one which preceded it, died decades ago. In its place, the political right can only offer some reversion to a rose-tinted imitation of the national economies which appeared to work so well during those years. The left, on the other hand, has bought into a weird faux-green post-truth techno-utopianism in which the world can be anything that one wishes it to be independent of such inconveniences as the laws of physics. Which is why, for example, we witness thousands of campaigners who couldn't live for more than a fortnight without fossil fuels, siding with a parasitic corporate "net-zero" non-solution which is more likely to lead to mass starvation and hypothermia than to the promised bright green techno-paradise.

What if Thiel is overly optimistic though? Might it be that the Club of Rome of which he was so critical was broadly correct? After all, the *Limits to Growth* was not an argument for or against progress, it was merely an attempt to use computing to model the effects of continuing in the way we had been up to the early 1970s. The result was unsettling.

The standard run saw global resources begin to deplete from the 1950s even as population and industrial output continued to grow into the first decades of the twenty-first century. But this "overshoot" produced a rapid decline in population, food and industry as the economy was forced to shrink back to a level allowed by the smaller resource

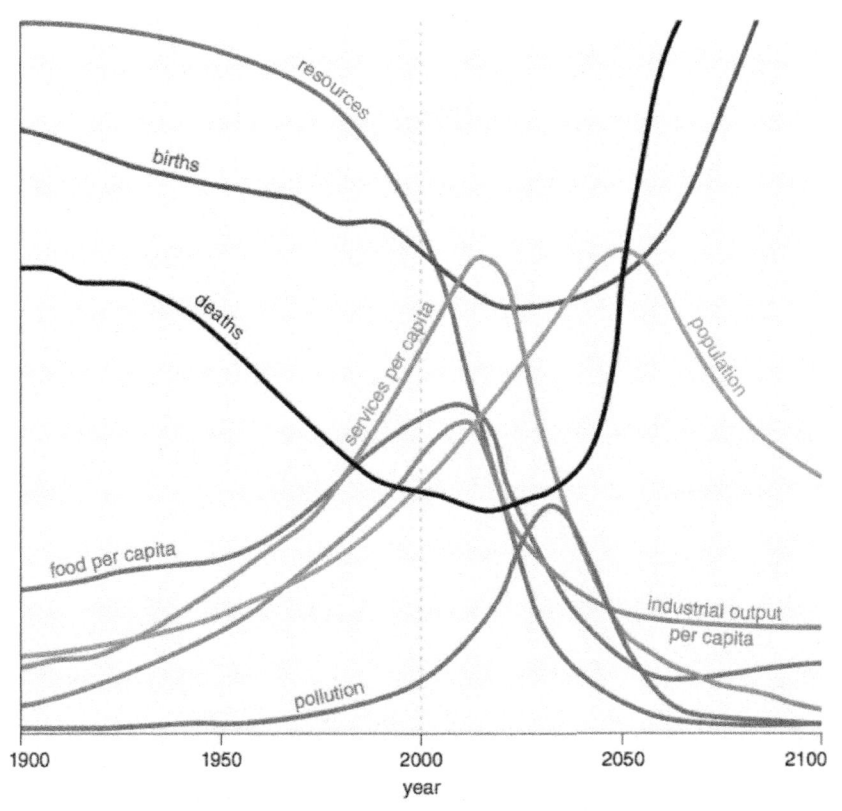

[Figure: Graph showing resources, births, deaths, population, food per capita, services per capita, industrial output per capita, and pollution from 1900 to 2100]

base. Recent reruns of the model[2], using today's access to far greater computing power, have led to very similar results, suggesting that we are currently at – or just past – the peak of industrial civilisation, and that pretty soon *everyone* will be going backward. And if this is so, then, far from living in an age of progress, industrialisation merely extended the upward section of the cycle of civilisation, allowing it to last much longer than Malthus could have possibly foreseen. Nevertheless, if we are now on the downslope of industrial civilisation – or at least the western version of it – might it be that the only question left to be resolved is how long our collapse is going to take?

Notes

1. Harrington, M. 25 July 2022. "Peter Thiel on the dangers of progress." *UnHerd*. https://unherd.com/2022/07/peter-thiel-on-the-dangers-of-progress

2. Meadows, D. and Randers, J. 2004. *Limits to Growth: The 30-Year Update*. Chelsea Green Publishing

Imagined Futures...

From the moment the first industrial machines arrived on the scene, people divided into two warring classes which are perhaps even more relevant today than they were at the dawn of industrial civilisation. Not the age-old division between capitalists and workers, but on one side, the adherents of the religion of progress, and on the other, those – like the Luddites or the followers of Captain Swing – who sought to maintain the craft skills of an earlier age. In the early years of the industrial age, the struggle was to prevent industrialisation from gathering pace. Today, as we pass the apex of industrial civilisation, we face movements which argue that industrialisation has gone too far and that we need to somehow turn the clock back. For some protestors, this means wiping away industrialisation entirely, plunging societies back to some imagined rural idyll... conveniently forgetting the day-to-day horrors – untreatable disease, periodic famine, infant death, low life-expectancy, etc. – that were the norm in pre-industrial economies. For most though, there is a desire for a sanitised, "green" post-industrialisation in which a host of digital technologies operated by machine learning AI, propel us into a virtualised techno-utopia.

An unsavoury conflict between capital and labour has, of course, rumbled on throughout the industrial age, despite establishment media claims that we have somehow transcended it. More realistically though, it is only the means by which the struggle is waged which has evolved over time. Initially, working people struggled *against* the inexorable transition to an industrial economy – against the enclosure of common land which left them destitute and against the automated factory machinery which undermined craft skills. And yet, wage labour became the only means of keeping a roof over the family's heads and putting food on the table. And so, thousands of the dispossessed were uprooted and moved to the new industrial towns.

Certainly, most capitalists tended to rally behind the narrative that industrialisation was a liberating force – freeing people from the drudgery of the medieval arrangements. There were even those, such as philanthropist Robert Owen – sometimes thought of as the father of British socialism[1] – who sought to improve the lot of the workforce, offering them a greater share of the profits than was generally available to industrial workers.

Arguments over the relative share of profits between capital and labour became the common point of protest and action once it was no longer possible to turn the clock back. While early industrialisation may have been liberating for the capitalist class and the small administrative class that it depended upon, for working people the experience was mostly negative. As Marx was to put it:

> "In handicrafts and manufacture, the workman makes use of a tool; in the factory, the machine makes use of him. There the movements of the instrument of labour proceed from him, here it is the movements of the machine that he must follow. In manufacture the workmen are parts of a living mechanism. In the factory we have a lifeless mechanism independent of the workman, who becomes its mere living appendage."

People may have been impoverished in pre-industrial village life, but prior to the twentieth century, it was hard to argue that industrialisation and urbanisation had been particularly liberating. Marx's collaborator Frederick Engels[2] – himself an industrialist – highlighted the plight of the urban working class:

> "I assert that thousands of industrious and worthy people – far worthier and more to be respected than all the rich of London – do find themselves in a condition unworthy

of human beings; and that every proletarian, everyone, without exception, is exposed to a similar fate without any fault of his own and in spite of every possible effort."

At the end of the nineteenth century, influential liberals Seebohm Rowntree[3] and Charles Booth[4] produced reports which fed directly into the social reforms introduced by the 1906 Liberal government. These attempted to apply a minimum standard below which nobody should be allowed to fall. The reforms also brought state intervention in the economy into being on a large scale for the first time – providing the political arena for the struggle over the relative share of the profits from industry. Indeed, the biggest success of the Liberal government was to wrest control of the state from the landed class in the House of Lords, establishing the primacy of the elected House of Commons.

By the beginning of the twentieth century, then, it appeared that industrialisation could be reformed – on both the economic and political fronts – to lift all classes up from the miseries of earlier ages. For in the march to automation, there was also the *promise* of liberation. The mass machinery of industry which had once turned people from skilled craft workers into mere machine minders had the *potential* to dispense with the need to labour at all. It was surely possible that in future almost all of our human needs and desires might be satisfied by entirely automated processes operated by machines barely touched by human hands. By the 1930s, economist John Maynard Keynes was predicting the arrival of a 15-hour-week, while Bertrand Russell[5] was writing in praise of idleness:

"From the beginning of civilization until the Industrial Revolution, a man could, as a rule, produce by hard work little more than was required for the subsistence of himself and his family, although his wife worked at least as hard as he did, and his children added their labour as soon as they were old enough to do so...

"Modern technique has made it possible to diminish enormously the amount of labour required to secure the necessaries of life for everyone. This was made obvious during the [1914-18] war. At that time all the men in the armed forces, and all the men and women engaged in the production of munitions, all the men and women engaged in spying, war propaganda, or Government offices connected with the war, were withdrawn from productive occupations. In spite of this, the general level of well-being among unskilled wage-earners on the side of the Allies was higher than before or since. The significance of this fact was concealed by finance: borrowing made it appear as if the future was nourishing the present. But that, of course, would have been impossible; a man cannot eat a loaf of bread that does not yet exist. The war showed conclusively that, by the scientific organization of production, it is possible to keep modern populations in fair comfort on a small part of the working capacity of the modern world."

There is some irony that Russell wrote this at a time when the mass unemployment of the Great Depression had led to the widespread use of soup kitchens – the 1930s version of today's foodbanks – to people so desperate that they agreed to work for meals rather than wages, and to the growing support of extremist political movements. Arguably though, those extremists were also promising some version of modernisation in which today's sacrifices pave the way for tomorrow's automated utopia. Recessionary periods though, are most likely to bring forth demands for a shorter working week precisely because they are times of high unemployment. We should not be surprised then, to find that similar sentiments came to the fore in the depression of the early 1980s – a period which also gave rise to a potential saviour in the shape of the emerging computing and communications sector. The embryonic utopia would be a world in which everything from the most mundane chore to the highest level technical or managerial function could be conducted by pre-programmed computers. Meanwhile, increasingly redundant humans would make a living selling personal services to one another in the course of a working week of no longer than 20 hours.

It might also come as no surprise to discover that during the debt-based boom of the 1990s and early 2000s, computers, the internet and mobile phones had merely become the latest machines that workers spent ever more of their time minding. This was the era of what David Graeber[6] referred to as "bullshit jobs" – roles that appeared to have little purpose other than enforcing conformity and servitude on those unfortunate enough to perform them. And after it all fell apart in 2008, those same workers found themselves putting in more hours than ever, even as their inflation-adjusted pay continued to fall.

The difference after 2008, is that unemployment barely exists in the way it had done in the early 1980s. Officially, anyone who works for an hour in any week is counted as being employed. The result is that until recently, the rate of unemployment has been at an all-time low. *Underemployment* – well that's a different matter. Far too many of us have been taking on two, three, or more part-time, zero-hours or gig-economy jobs in an attempt to approximate a decent weekly wage. And for some 4.8 million of us, wages are still so low that we have to turn to Universal Credit to top-up incomes to a level that is still borderline inhumane.

It comes as no surprise then, that once again we see various utopias being proposed, to allow digital technology and AI to take up the slack while allowing people to enjoy more leisure time funded by a universal basic income. From the political left comes a techno-communism envisaged by activists such as Aaron Bastani[7], who draws on a raft of yet-to-be-invented technologies which will supposedly set us free once we have overthrown the dead hand of a decaying capitalist class which is out of answers. The current moment of "Third Disruption," we are told, is the latest major revolution in the upward arc of human progress – the first being the development of agriculture, and the second the industrial revolution:

> "'Communism' is used here for the benefit of precision; the intention being to denote a society in which work is eliminated, scarcity replaced by abundance and where labour and leisure blend into one another. Given the possibilities arising from the Third Disruption, with the emergence of extreme supply in information, labour, energy and resources, it should be viewed not only as an idea adequate to our time but impossible before now. [Fully Automated Luxury Communism] does not underpin the trends of the Third Disruption – it is their conclusion... If we want it."

There are remarkable similarities with the ruling technocracy's version of techno-utopia which goes under such titles as, "The Great Reset," "The Green New Deal," or the "Fourth Industrial Revolution." This is not entirely surprising since this proposed future is also collectivist in nature although in more of a fascistic than socialistic manner. Far from the people rising up and seizing control, The Great Reset is about impowering the technocracy to exercise digital control over a supposedly uneducated, backward, and unwilling populace in order to force it to accept a new way of life which will be in its long-term interest.

Both left and right techno-utopian visions are intended as palatable solutions to a bottleneck of crises which threaten to throw civilisation into reverse unless something is done. The biggest of these by far, in the eyes of both camps, is environmental, and demands that we reshape our entire way of life so that we may transition from dirty fossil fuels to clean green alternatives like solar, wind, and geothermal electricity generation. This is where the Green New Deal element comes in. The switch to a fully digitised electrified economy requires far more than simply building out the renewable energy infrastructure... although this is a monumental task in itself. Everything that we currently do – from delivering goods to heating our homes and from flying to our holidays to growing our food – will also have to be digitised and electrified. Nevertheless, the true believers argue that *almost* all of the technology required to make this happen already exists, and that the exponentially increasing speed of computing and communications means that the few technologies yet to be invented will be putting in an appearance any day now.

It is this huge faith in the power of computing and communications which lies behind all of the techno-utopian futures – irrespective of the political ideologies of those proposing them. The point of unity is that we are in the midst of a *technological* revolution[8]:

> "We have yet to grasp fully the speed and breadth of this new revolution. Consider the unlimited possibilities of having billions of people connected by mobile devices, giving rise to unprecedented processing power, storage capabilities and knowledge access. Or think about the staggering confluence of emerging technology breakthroughs, covering wide-ranging fields such as artificial intelligence (AI), robotics, the internet of things (IoT), autonomous vehicles, 3D printing, nanotechnology, biotechnology, materials science, energy storage and quantum computing, to name a few. Many of these innovations are in their infancy, but they are already reaching an inflection point in their development as they build on and amplify each other in

a fusion of technologies across the physical, digital and biological worlds."

The outcome – whether we choose to be led there by the self-identifying activist vanguard of the proletariat or by a neofascist technocracy – is a melding of work and leisure, in which the drudgery of life is carried out by machines even as humans develop and trade their innate creative potential. Ida Auken[9], a Danish politician and contributor to the World Economic Forum, offered a much-derided vision of the coming brave new world:

> "It might seem odd to you, but it makes perfect sense for us in this city. Everything you considered a product, has now become a service. We have access to transportation, accommodation, food and all the things we need in our daily lives. One by one all these things became free, so it ended up not making sense for us to own much.
>
> "First communication became digitized and free to everyone. Then, when clean energy became free, things started to move quickly. Transportation dropped dramatically in price. It made no sense for us to own cars anymore, because we could call a driverless vehicle or a flying car for longer journeys within minutes. We started transporting ourselves in a much more organized and coordinated way when public transport became easier, quicker and more convenient than the car. Now I can hardly believe that we accepted congestion and traffic jams, not to mention the air pollution from combustion engines. What were we thinking?"

Utopian indeed! And the critics soon retitled it "you'll own nothing and be happy," painting a picture of a totally surveilled Huxleyan future in which the technocracy – or rather its automated algorithms – had total control over every aspect of people's lives. If you thought being banned from Twitter or Facebook was a big deal, imagine how life is going to be when the technocracy can suspend your bank account because you said something they disapproved of, or when you are confined to your house because you failed to get your vaccine status updated on your health app. Even if the upward arc of progress, which the disciples of the techno-utopian future believe in, turns out to be true, if history is our guide, the odds surely favour the forces of tyranny over those of human flourishing. After all, the freedoms of association and speech which were previously the preserve only of the elite classes of the ancient world, only became commonplace in a select handful of wealthy Western states. And only then for what, in the 200,000-year sweep of human existence, has been no more than the blink of an eye. Even if Herr Schwab and his inner circle regard themselves as benign tyrants, tyrants they remain. And one day soon they will be replaced by a new generation of technocratic rulers who pay far less regard to the plight of their minions.

There is more to this though. For all of the claim of environmentalism, the techno-utopias share an implicit attempt to disconnect humanity from the physical world entirely. Why else would they imagine extremely expensive laboratory-grown artificial meat replacing perfectly good cows, sheep and pigs which, farmed in the right way, help to regenerate soils which have been worn out by excessive fertiliser use? There is, perhaps something about the class from which these techno-utopians emerge which causes an innate anti-Gaian urge to control all and to destroy all which cannot be controlled. As Christopher Lasch observed:

> "The thinking classes are fatally removed from the physical side of life... Their only relation to productive labor is that of consumers. They have no experience of making anything substantial or enduring. They live in a world of abstractions and images, a simulated world that consists of computerized models of reality – "hyperreality," as it's been called – as distinguished from the palatable, immediate, physical reality inhabited by

ordinary men and women. Their belief in "social construction of reality" – the central dogma of postmodernist thought – reflects the experience of living in an artificial environment from which everything that resists human control (unavoidably, everything familiar and reassuring as well) has been rigorously excluded. Control has become their obsession. In their drive to insulate themselves against risk and contingency – against the unpredictable hazards that afflict human life – the thinking classes have seceded not just from the common world around them but from reality itself."

The new manifestation of the old antagonism between capital and labour morphs into a divide between "physicals" and "virtuals." As Mary Harrington explains[10]:

"What's key is that the moral outlook is downstream of concrete material interests. Physicals work in sectors such as farming, construction, manufacturing, haulage, mining, and so on: occupations inextricable from the material world. Virtuals, on the other hand, work at a layer of abstraction apart from the physical world: think finance, academia, education, media, tech, and so on.

"And Virtuals dominate the elite. For as the West has de-industrialised, Western money and power have drained from Physical occupations toward Virtual ones such as finance and tech. And, as a consequence, Virtuals today hold a near-monopoly on institutional power...

"Still, it remains to be seen whether the Virtuals' dominance really is as complete as it appears from their stranglehold on government and the media. At the last count, Virtuals remain materially dependent on the real economy: without farm workers, shop workers, bin men and drivers, the laptop class are as helpless and useless as a snail without its shell. This was visible in those groups for whom lockdown rules were most blithely waived: despite often-cramped living conditions, for example, even those seasonal agricultural workers coming to the UK from high-risk countries were exempted from the 14-day quarantine rule."

The distinction maps far more closely to the Brexit/Remain divide in the UK and to the Trump/Clinton divide in the USA, than does a traditional working class v upper class mapping. Moreover, the physicals v virtuals divide closely superimposes onto David Goodhart's somewhere v anywhere[11] which did a great deal to clarify the drivers behind the Brexit referendum results:

> "The old distinctions of class and economic interest have not disappeared but are increasingly over-laid by a larger and looser one—between the people who see the world from Anywhere and the people who see it from Somewhere.
>
> "Anywheres dominate our culture and society. They tend to do well at school—Vernon Bogdanor calls them the 'exam-passing classes'—then usually move from home to a residential university in their late teens and on to a career in the professions that might take them to London or even abroad for a year or two. Such people have portable 'achieved' identities, based on educational and career success which makes them generally comfortable and confident with new places and people.
>
> "Somewheres are more rooted and usually have 'ascribed' identities—Scottish farmer, working class Geordie, Cornish housewife—based on group belonging and particular places, which is why they often find rapid change more unsettling. One core group of Somewheres have been called the 'left behind'—mainly older white working class men with little education. They have lost economically with the decline of well-paid jobs for people without qualifications and culturally, too, with the disappearance of a distinct working-class culture and the marginalisation of their views in the public conversation.

> However, Somewhere ambivalence about recent social trends spreads far beyond this group and is shared by many in all social classes, especially the least mobile. Despite recent increases in geographical mobility, about 60 per cent of British people still live within 20 miles of where they lived when they were fourteen."

Just as the anywhere/virtuals can include large numbers of white-collar working class people sat behind computers in call centres, so the somewhere/physicals can include the relatively affluent owners and managers of factories and farms. What matters is the connection – or lack thereof – to what we might call the "real" economy and, indeed, the real world. And it explains to a large extent why the technocracy – particularly that part of it which has captured the cultural heights – actively despises anything which reminds them that, like it or not, they are still flesh and blood and that their wished-for utopia must still operate within the parameters of the physical universe.

More than this though, it is surely the increasingly obvious retreat from progress which makes the flight into techno-utopian fantasy all the greater. The millions of ordinary people – more a precariat than a proletariat these days – so despised by the technocracy stand as living and breathing evidence of the failure of education and meritocracy to solve even one of the great socio-economic ills which the technocracy was supposed to have the answers to. Most people today are poorer and less secure than their parents had been. And progress, insofar as it was real at all, appears only to have been a brief, post-war flash in the pan before the dead hand of poverty and inequality returned.

Notes

1. See, e.g., MacEwen, T. undated. "Robert Owen, Father of British Socialism." *History Magazine.* www.historic-uk.com/HistoryUK/HistoryofWales/Robert-Owen-Father-British-Socialsm

2. Engels, F. 1845. *The Condition of the Working-class in England in 1844.* P31

3. Rowntree, S. 1901. Poverty, *A Study of Town Life*

4. Booth, C. (ed) 1893. *Life and Labour of the People in London*

5. Russel, B. 2004. *In Praise of Idleness: And Other Essays.* Routledge; 2nd edition. pp4-6

6. Graeber, D. 2018. *Bullshit Jobs: A Theory.* Penguin

7. Bastani, A. 2019. *Fully Automated Luxury Communism: A Manifesto.* Verso

8. Schwab, K. 2016. *The Fourth Industrial Revolution.* WEF. P7

9. Auken, I. 10 November 2016. "Welcome To 2030: I Own Nothing, Have No Privacy And Life Has Never Been Better." *Forbes.* https://www.forbes.com/sites/worldeconomicforum/2016/11/10/shopping-i-cant-really-remember-what-that-is-or-how-differently-well-live-in-2030/

10. Harrington, M. 26 October 2022. "Can Sunak end the new class war? A deep divide exists between Virtuals and Physicals." *UnHerd.* https://unherd.com/2022/10/can-sunak-end-the-new-class-war

11. Goodhart, D. 2017. *The Road to Somewhere: The New Tribes Shaping British Politics.* Penguin

... and hard realities

No matter how diverse the politics behind them, all of the imagined "green," hi-tech futures share one crucial feature – they all omit any calculation of the resources, energy and time required to construct them. How much copper, for example, would be required to construct the proposed brave new world? Not just in uprating electricity grids to accommodate the more diffused renewable energy generation, but also to refashion all of our transport, industry and agriculture to wean us off fossil fuels. That is just one resource. How much steel, aluminium, concrete and plastic are going to be needed to build out the massive numbers of wind turbines and solar panels that are required? Is this to be done solely using renewable *electricity*, or are we to use fossil fuels to build out this new infrastructure? If the latter, where are we going to get these additional fossil fuels? And how much are they going to cost? Indeed, how much time is it going to take to achieve?

The politicians, economists, and bankers driving the official version of the Great Green New Reset seem to think that it can be completed by 2050 – just 28 years from now – and that the transportation component can be implemented by 2030 – just eight years from now! This, I think, says more about the abject imbecility of politicians, economists, and bankers than it does about the likely success of this final "great project" of the industrial age. Because, while targets have been set and financial structures altered accordingly, only a handful of people worldwide have even begun to calculate the energy and resources required to realise these aims. And even if they are being woefully pessimistic, the bottom line remains that the goal is impossible to reach... and we may end up killing billions of people trying to reach it.

Professor Richard Herrington from the UK National History Museum says the task is impossible[1]. He and his colleagues began to calculate the mineral resources likely to be required just for the UK portion of the proposed transition. The results were far from favourable:

"To replace all UK-based vehicles today with electric vehicles (not including the LGV and HGV fleets), assuming they use the most resource-frugal next-generation NMC 811 batteries, would take 207,900 tonnes cobalt, 264,600 tonnes of lithium carbonate (LCE), at least 7,200 tonnes of neodymium and dysprosium, in addition to 2,362,500 tonnes copper. This represents, just under two times the total annual world cobalt production, nearly the entire world production of neodymium, three quarters the world's lithium production and at least half of the world's copper production during 2018. Even ensuring the annual supply of electric vehicles only, from 2035 as pledged, will require the UK to annually import the equivalent of the entire annual cobalt needs of European industry...

"If wind farms are chosen to generate the power for the projected two billion cars at UK average usage, this requires the equivalent of a further years' worth of total global copper supply and 10 years' worth of global neodymium and dysprosium production to build the windfarms.

"Solar power is also problematic – it is also resource hungry; all the photovoltaic systems currently on the market are reliant on one or more raw materials classed as 'critical' or 'near critical' by the EU and/or US Department of Energy (high purity silicon, indium, tellurium, gallium) because of their natural scarcity or their recovery as minor-by-products of other commodities...

"Both these wind turbine and solar generation options for the added electrical power generation capacity have substantial demands for steel, aluminium, cement and glass."

Professor Simon Michaux from the Geological Survey of Finland goes much further in setting out the likely resource implications of a transition from fossil fuels to a combination of renewable and nuclear energy. In a 1,000-page technical assessment[2], Michaux calculates the energy mix required to phase out fossil fuels, and the resource implications that this will have:

> "A novel bottom-up approach (as opposed to the typical top-down approach) was used to make the calculations presented here. Previous studies have also tended to focus on estimated costs of production and CO2 footprint metrics, whereas the present report is based on the physical material requirements...
>
> "Calculations reported here suggest that the total additional non-fossil fuel electrical power annual capacity to be added to the global grid will need to be around 37,670.6 TWh. If the same non-fossil fuel energy mix as that reported in 2018 is assumed, then this translates into an extra 221,594 new power plants will be needed to be constructed and commissioned. To put this in context, the total power plant fleet in 2018 (all types including fossil fuel plants) was only 46,423 stations. This large number reflects the lower Energy Returned on Energy Invested (ERoEI) ratio of renewable power compared to current fossil fuels."

Starting from the bottom-up, Michaux calculates the resource requirements of each of the required technologies based on 2018 (i.e., pre-pandemic) efficiency, and then multiplies these up according to the numbers required to replace fossil fuels in the global economy. The calculations are likely conservative as, for example, they do not include the on-site fossil fuel used by industry to generate heat. Nor do they include all of the additional grid infrastructure which would be required to connect the current national and transnational grids in order to move electricity from where it is generated to where it is needed. Nevertheless, the conclusions are stark:

Metal	Element	Total metal required produce one generation of technology units to phase out fossil fuels (tonnes)	Global Metal Production 2019 (tonnes)	Years to produce metal at 2019 rates of production (years)
Copper	Cu	4 575 523 674	24 200 000	189,1
Nickel	Ni	940 578 114	2 350 142	400,2
Lithium	Li	944 150 293	95 170 *	9920,7
Cobalt	Co	218 396 990	126 019	1733,0
Graphite (natural flake)	C	8 973 640 257	1 156 300 ♦	3287,9
Graphite (synthetic)	C		1 573 000 ♦	-
Silicon (Metallurgical)	Si	49 571 460	8 410 000	5,9
Vanadium	V	681 865 986	96 021 *	7101,2
Rare Earth Metals	-			
Neodymium	Nd	965 183	23 900	40,4
Germanium	Ge	4 163 162	143	29113,0
Lanthanum	La	5 970 738	35 800	166,8
Praseodymium	Pr	235 387	7 500	31,4
Dysprosium	Dy	196 207	1 000	196,2
Terbium	Tb	16 771	280	59,9

* Estimated from mining production. All other values are refining production values.
♦ Natural flake graphite and synthetic graphite was combined to estimate total production

Looking at the resources which would be needed to build just the first generation of the technologies required to transition from fossil fuels to renewable energy, it becomes obvious that we would need, somehow, to be able to mine the entire solar system, because there is nowhere close to enough on planet Earth. Taking just copper – which is a key ingredient to any and every electrical technology – we would require 189 years' worth to build out the new infrastructure. But we don't have centuries or even decades because – for both environmental and thermodynamic reasons – we have to develop whatever our alternative energy system is going to be in just years. And copper is one of the more abundant resources. Any widespread use of batteries is scuppered by the lack of lithium – we would require 9,920 years' worth of that. We also need an eye-watering 29,113 years' worth of Germanium – a semiconductor used in transistors and other electronic technologies.

Even if, as some critics suggest – although none gives their own calculation – Michaux is being too pessimistic, the bottom line remains that there is simply not enough of planet Earth to allow us to continue operating the current version of an advanced, globalised economy with any mix of alternatives to fossil fuels... which, among other things, are also the only viable energy source for mining all of those mineral resources we require. Moreover, even if we did *construct* a fraction of the alternative energy technologies needed to move toward the imagined techno-utopia, we have yet to calculate the energy and resources required to *deploy* and *maintain* them.

Most techno-utopian proposals duck this issue by claiming that it is somehow possible to "decouple" economic growth from energy and resources. Again, however, no serious evidence has been produced to back up the claim, while serious scientists point to its impossibility. For example, Ward et. Al[3]. explain that:

> "GDP ultimately cannot plausibly be decoupled from growth in material and energy use, demonstrating categorically that GDP growth cannot be sustained indefinitely. It is therefore misleading to develop growth-oriented policy around the expectation that decoupling is possible... The mounting costs of 'uneconomic growth' suggest that the pursuit of decoupling–if it were possible– in order to sustain GDP growth would be a misguided effort...
>
> "If GDP growth as a societal goal is unsustainable, then it is ultimately necessary for nations and the world to transition to a steady or declining GDP scenario. We

contend that it will be easier to start this transition now while there is still capacity for technological gains, rather than go down the path of decoupling and be forced to make a transition post 2050 when we are closer to the theoretical limits to technological efficiency gains. We argue that now is the time to recognize the biophysical limits, and to begin the overdue task of re-orienting society around a more achievable and satisfying set of goals than simply growing forever."

Given the impact of two years of lockdown disruption, resulting in broken supply chains and energy shortages, the proposed 2050 limit is likely optimistic... 2030 may turn out to be more realistic, not least because, in the pursuit of some version of a fourth industrial revolution, public policy across the western world is actively discouraging further investment in fossil fuel production even though we are still a *very* long way from developing the proposed replacements. For all of the funding and resources which have been ploughed into NRREHTs like wind, solar, tide, wave and geothermal, they account for less than five percent of our energy consumption, and still lag far behind hydroelectric and nuclear power. Indeed, coal, gas, and oil still account for more than eighty percent of our energy consumption and remain crucial to the agriculture, critical industry, and transportation that we depend upon for life support.

Notice, by the way, that with the exception of the oil shocks of the 1970s, the collapse of the Soviet Union in 1991, and the Covid lockdowns, our energy consumption has been growing exponentially. As such, NRREHTs have not been *replacing* fossil fuels, they have merely been added to the mix. The result is that, with less than three decades to go, we have not even begun the process of ending our dependence on fossil fuels.

Global primary energy consumption by source

Primary energy is calculated based on the 'substitution method' which takes account of the inefficiencies in fossil fuel production by converting non-fossil energy into the energy inputs required if they had the same conversion losses as fossil fuels.

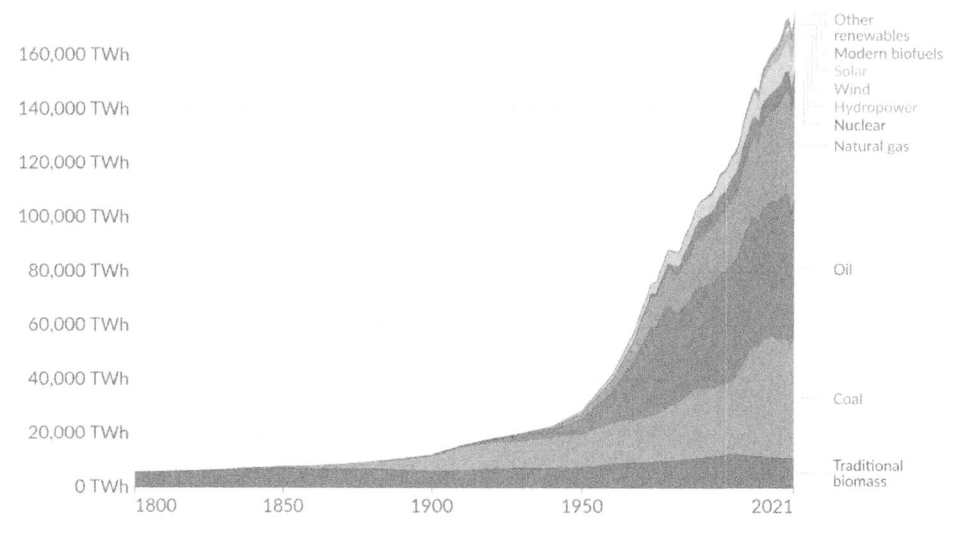

Source: Our World in Data based on Vaclav Smil (2017) and BP Statistical Review of World Energy — OurWorldInData.org/energy • CC BY

In raw terms, to phase out fossil fuels requires that we install some 136,000 terawatt hours per year from alternative sources. That's the equivalent of just over 34,000 Hornsea – currently the biggest in the world – wind farms. That works out at 24 Hornsea equivalent wind farms *every week*! between January 2023 and January 2050. Consider that Hornsea itself was first proposed in 2008 and is only now completing its third phase. Of course, wind is not the only low-carbon option. A growing number of techno-utopians recognise this and are coming around to nuclear as an important part of the future energy mix. So how many nuclear power plants would we need to build to reach the 2050 net zero goal? If we take the big Hinkley Point C, third-generation station currently being built in southwest England, which is expected to provide 26 TWh when it comes on stream in 2028... or so, then we would need to build 5,231 between now and 2050. That's 3.7 Hinkley C power plants *per week*! Again, consider that Hinkley C was first mooted in 2010, with the licence granted in 2012. It was supposed to come online in 2026 but is several years behind schedule. A duplicate power plant to be located at Sizewell on the east coast of England has only just been given the go ahead.

The costs involved are eye-watering too. Hinkley Point C is currently expected to come in at around £26 billion. The final, four phase, Hornsea offshore wind farm is less expensive at some £4.2 billion, but that's still £142,800,000,000,000 that *someone* would have to stump up. And that's before we begin to think about the battery, hydro and/or gravity back-up which would have to be installed to iron-out the intermittency which bedevils NRREHTs. And then there's the problem of electrification itself.

Some technologies and economic sectors lend themselves to electrification. Small cars and scooters, for example are much simpler to build and maintain than their internal combustion alternatives – although, as we have seen, there is simply not enough of Planet Earth to allow us to swap *every* or even *most* cars and scooters with their battery-electric alternatives. And once we move to larger and more often diesel-powered vehicles, there is simply no viable battery technology to overcome the power to weight problem. We can, for example, operate relatively small lorries and buses on local transport routes (where regenerative braking increases range) using batteries and electric motors. But long-haul trucks and long-distance coaches and trains cannot carry the weight of batteries that would be required without losing freight and/or passenger capacity. Hydrogen fuel cells might offer a solution. Although most hydrogen is reformed from natural gas and, in any case, presents a raft of storage problems of its own. Again, we will see *some* hydrogen cell-powered vehicles but there is no way we get to swap out all or even most of the vehicles we currently power with diesel.

Industrial heat raises a more difficult problem again. Currently, two of the four essential materials for maintaining the modern economy – steel and cement – and without which, alternatives to fossil fuels are impossible to construct, require a degree of heat which can only be provided by burning fossil fuels – mostly coal and gas. Some *theoretical* alternatives to burning coal in steel foundries have been proposed (although coke – refined carbon from coal – is still an essential ingredient of the steel itself) but no scalable version has been demonstrated yet.

Plastic – another of the essential materials – is an even more difficult problem because it is a by-product of oil and gas. This points to a complexity within the oil industry which most techno-utopian proposals overlook. An average barrel of oil – and barrels vary considerably in gravity depending upon their source – provides around 40 percent petrol (gasoline), 30 percent diesel and aviation fuel, five percent shipping oil, and 25 percent by-products such as chemical feedstocks, lubricants and asphalt. We cannot just have one product – such as the chemical feedstock to produce plastic – but do away with all of the others. Oil refineries simply don't work that way. Indeed, in a sense, the petrol that we ordinary workers and consumers use for private motoring helps to subsidise those oil products – like diesel and plastic – which are essential to our way of life. If demand for petrol falls, the cost of the more essential products rises and – less obviously – petrol becomes a waste product that must somehow be disposed of.

Nitrogen fertiliser is the fourth and, perhaps least, essential material insofar as modern industrial agriculture depends upon a steady and *cheap* supply to maintain the yields needed to feed eight billion people. As we are finding out to our cost just at the moment – with sky-high gas prices making fertiliser too expensive for many farmers – it is impossible to maintain short-term yields without artificial fertiliser. Longer-term, of course, there is growing evidence in favour of a shift to regenerative agriculture which, given time, might match the yields currently obtained using artificial fertilisers. Getting from where we are to where we might choose to be though, *without widespread famine*, remains a serious problem.

Much else that we take for granted about the modern world, from mobile phones to dental anaesthetic and from warm clothing to clean drinking water, requires fossil fuels in its manufacture and/or supply. And nobody has put forward a serious proposal for how we might develop acceptable, non-fossil fuel alternatives.

In short, as Charles Hall puts it, if we were marking the various proposed techno-utopias as answers to an exam paper, while we might afford them an 'A' for creativity and imagination, we would have to give them an 'F' for their lack of grounding in reality... and especially for their failure to conform to the laws of physics.

So, is the answer that we continue with business as usual?

This, unfortunately, is where our predicament gets seriously scary. Because the *surplus* energy that we derive from fossil fuels has been declining for decades and is the main reason why we have reeled from one economic crisis to another since the mid-1970s. This is not because we are "running out" of fossil fuel. Indeed, there is probably as much oil still in the Earth's crust as all of the oil we have consumed since the dawn of the industrial revolution. The problem is that we appear to have passed the peak of global output toward the end of 2018 – although the picture has been distorted by two-years of lockdown and the ensuing shortages. This, in turn throws up several related issues concerning the way in which we produced oil in the past.

The gradual decline in oil production need not, in and of itself, result in a crisis. There are many frivolous ways in which we continue to burn oil. And so, we *could* switch further consumption only to those activities which are essential to the continued operation of our advanced and complex way of life. This is deceptive though. Because our current, so-called "fiat," monetary system depends upon credit to grow the supply of currency. That is, on the international stage, banks simply create dollars out of thin air when they issue dollar denominated loans. The same thing happens in national economies, where banks create the indigenous currency when they make loans. In the UK, for example, more than 97 percent of the pounds in circulation were created by private banks in the form of "bank credit." So here's the problem, if currency is created as debt, it comes with interest attached. So where do we find the currency to repay the debt *and the interest*? In short, we have to borrow it.

Internationally and nationally, the debt-based currency system dictates that we must keep borrowing currency into existence in order to pay off the outstanding debt plus the interest. But banks do not just loan currency for no good reason. Rather, they loan currency to invest in the economy or to allow households to consume things – which is where businesses recover the currency needed to repay their debts. And so, if the amount of currency needed at any time *must* be bigger than the amount previously borrowed, businesses and households (collectively) must produce and consume ever more stuff – which requires ever more energy and resources – in order to avoid a 2008-style economic crash. In short, the monetary system requires *exponential* economic growth.

In the age of coal – starting with the first British beam engines in the early eighteenth century and ending sometime in the 1920s – coal production growth was slow.

It is only from the end of the nineteenth century, as first Germany and later the USA overtook British industrial output, that global coal production and consumption grew

Global primary energy consumption by source

Primary energy is calculated based on the 'substitution method' which takes account of the inefficiencies in fossil fuel production by converting non-fossil energy into the energy inputs required if they had the same conversion losses as fossil fuels.

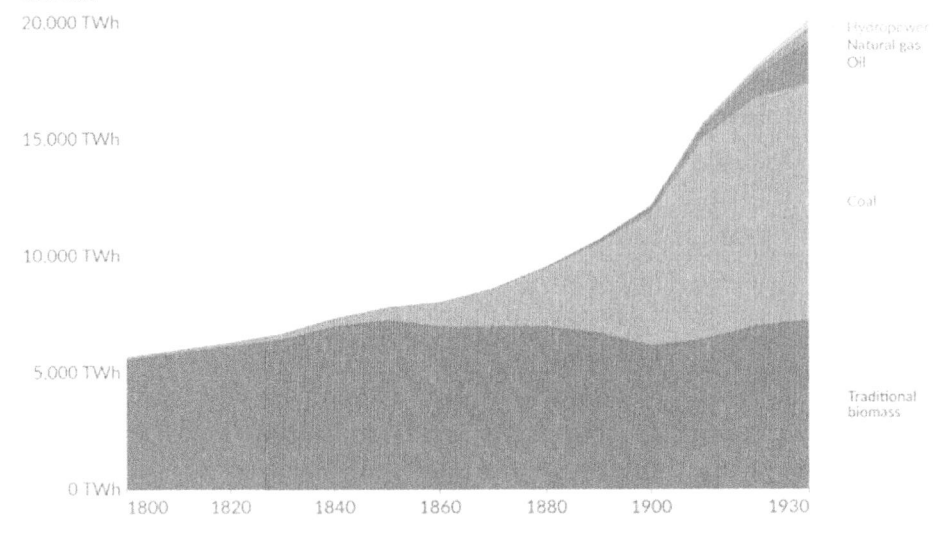

[Stacked area chart from 1800 to 1930 showing global primary energy consumption in TWh, with categories from top to bottom: Hydropower, Natural gas, Oil, Coal, Traditional biomass. Y-axis ranges from 0 TWh to 20,000 TWh.]

Source: Our World in Data based on Vaclav Smil (2017) and BP Statistical Review of World Energy. OurWorldinData.org/energy • CC BY

rapidly. The period after the First World War saw a big uptick in coal growth before *the rate of* growth began to slow in the 1920s... precipitating the financial crisis which resulted in the Great depression of the 1930s. In effect, the world had reached the peak of *coal-based* coal growth. So that, if coal had been the only fossil fuel, industrial civilisation would have begun to collapse back then. There was though, an even more energy-dense and versatile fossil fuel waiting in the wings. Oil – and especially the European and Japanese economies' transition from coal to oil after the Second World War – ushered in a golden age of prosperity as oil production and consumption grew exponentially between 1953 and 1973. As historian Paul Kennedy explains[4]:

> "The accumulated world industrial output between 1953 and 1973 was comparable in volume to that of the entire century and a half which separated 1953 from 1800. The recovery of war-damaged economies, the development of new technologies, the continued shift from agriculture

to industry, the harnessing of national resources within 'planned economies,' and the spread of industrialization to the Third World all helped to effect this dramatic change. In an even more emphatic way, and for much the same reasons, the volume of world trade also grew spectacularly after 1945..."

Although partially artificial, 1973 marked the end of the period of exponential oil growth. The OPEC oil embargo in October 1973 brought forward the end of exponential growth by a few years. But continental US oil production had peaked in 1970 – one reason OPEC was emboldened to embargo the western economies. Moreover, the gold-backed Bretton Woods currency system had also failed, causing the Nixon Administration to end the link between the dollar and gold to which the other global currencies were tied.

As had happened with coal in the 1920s, oil production continued to rise. But growth was far slower, putting an end to the post-war economic boom and ushering in a period marred by ever deeper economic crises:

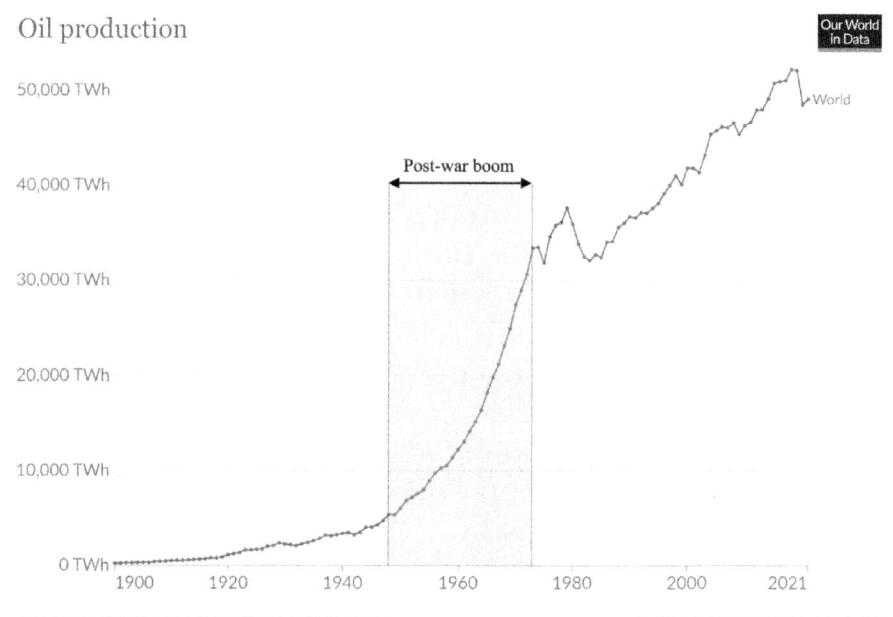

Oil production

Source: BP Statistical Review of World Energy; the Shift Project   OurWorldinData.org/fossil-fuels/ • CC BY

One reason for our inability to push production higher is due to the way the oil industry developed. The first oil fields were within the continental USA. And while the TV comedy *The Beverley Hill Billies* may have exaggerated the ease with which oil could be produced – the lead character accidentally fires a shotgun round into the ground and oil spurts out – production involved little more than hammering a pipe a few meters into the ground to allow large volumes of pressurised oil to gush to the surface.

Initially, US oil was used to produce kerosene as a replacement to fast depleting whale oil for lighting – the unregulated disposal of the remaining oil products taking a huge toll on the local environment. But even before large oil deposits had been tapped, patents existed for gas and liquid internal combustion engines. These began replacing horses, helping to convert the carriage-making industry in Detroit – at the Mississippi end of the Great Lakes trade route – into the world's first automobile industry.

Oil drove demand for cars and trucks, which, in turn, drove demand for ever more oil. And the USA was blessed with vast quantities. While Romanian, Persian, and Caucasian deposits kept the economies of Europe from imploding in the 1930s, in order to win the Second World War, the European allies were obliged to turn to the USA to power their armed forces to eventual victory. In the course of the war, the USA provided six out of every seven barrels of oil consumed. Venezuela and the Caucuses supplied much of what was left. And the key reason Germany lost was that its Romanian and Hungarian oil was insufficient to running even its peacetime economy – Germany could produce some of the most technically-advanced aeroplanes and tanks but having failed to capture (or at least capture intact) the oil fields in the Caucasus, the fuel-starved German military was forced onto the defensive.

Just as Britain had been the first country to exploit coal *and* the first to hit peak production (in 1913), so the USA's *conventional* oil production peaked in 1970. US producers might have done more to increase production at that point, except that by the 1970s the vast oil deposits of the Middle East and North Africa were in production – often with the support of the same US oil corporations. There was little point investing in expensive oil extraction in declining US deposits when there were big profits to be made on the other side of the Atlantic.

The OPEC oil embargo, the Iran-Iraq War and the economic crises they gave rise to, changed the thinking for states and oil corporations alike. Energy security became an issue. But it was the higher price of oil in the 1970s which led to the opening up of new, offshore fields in Alaska, the North Sea and the Gulf of Mexico. It was these – more expensive to produce – deposits which provided the corporate profits and state tax incomes which drove the final, debt-based economic boom in the western economies between 1995 and 2005.

The reason the *global* economy began to slow from 2005 was that *conventional* oil production – which encompasses almost all of the giant oil fields on Earth – had peaked. Prices began to rise, causing a supply-side shock across the economy as everything made from or transported with oil began to increase in price. This was not "inflation" in the true meaning of the word – an expansion of the currency supply which causes prices to rise. Rather, as Frank Shostak from the Mises Institute points out[5]:

> "If the price of oil goes up and if people continue to use the same amount of oil as before then this means that people are now forced to allocate more money for oil. If people's money stock remains unchanged then this means that less money is available for other goods and services, all other things being equal. This of course

implies that the average price of other goods and services must come off.

"Note that the overall money spent on goods does not change. Only the composition of spending has altered here, with more on oil and less on other goods. Hence, the average price of goods or money per unit of good remains unchanged."

Central bankers thought differently, implementing the interest rate rises which pulled the rug out from beneath the mountain of debt which had been accumulated since the 1990s, and undermining billions of dollars of derivatives based upon the anticipated income from that debt. The result was the banking and financial failure of 2008... a failure which has never been repaired.

The American shale bubble was a somewhat unexpected consequence of the post-2008 banking and financial landscape. Gone were the happy days when people couldn't open their front doors because of the mountain of pre-approved loan offers. Businesses struggled to find investment at affordable interest rates. And, crucially, with interest rates close to zero, investors struggled to find a return on their investments. The existence of the shale deposits and the technical means of drilling and hydraulically fracturing them had been around for decades. The reason nobody had drilled them up until then was that they were far too expensive. After 2008 though, world oil prices shot up. And even though investment in fracking was risky, the potential returns were huge. And so, Wall Street set about spending billions of dollars to produce millions of dollars' worth of shale oil, thereby flooding the world market and bringing oil prices back down to around $30 per barrel.

Although we tend to think of costs in currency terms, the real issue concerns the *energy* cost of producing energy. In the early years of the twentieth century, oil companies could produce hundreds of barrels for every one barrel (of oil equivalent) invested in production. But over time, this energy cost rose so that, by the time the world turned to deep sea deposits, tar sands and shale oil, the energy return on energy invested (EROEI) was, in some cases at least, less than the 10-15 to one required to maintain a modern industrial economy:

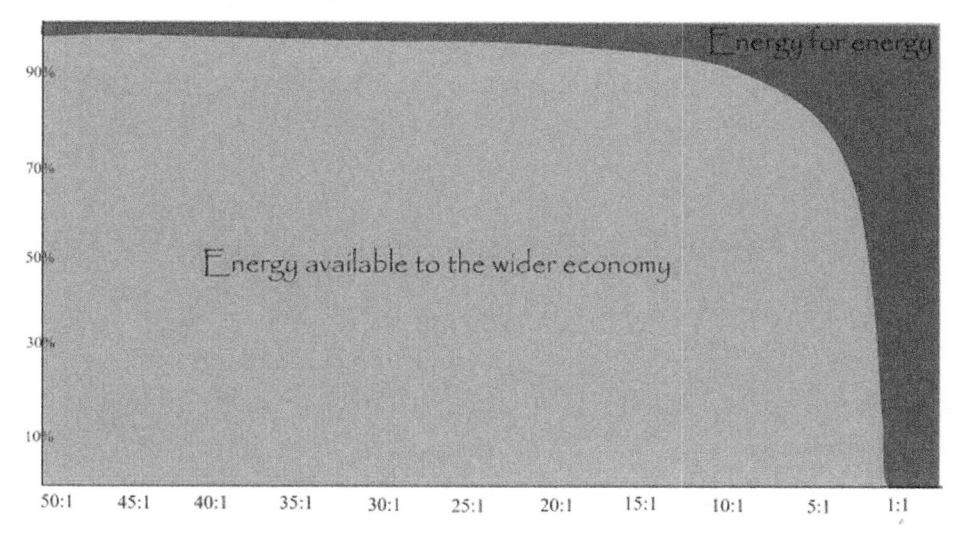

[Chart showing "Energy for energy" and "Energy available to the wider economy", with y-axis from 10% to 90% and x-axis ratios from 50:1 to 1:1]

Much of the discussion around EROEI is illustrative. There is no agreed means of measuring EROEI, and those academics who have attempted it have been criticised for what they left out. For example, much of the "energy" which has to be invested is "embodied" in all of the infrastructure, equipment and tools needed for production. But it is all but impossible to calculate this input. Similarly, some cut off point is needed on the "energy-out" side of the calculation. All too often this is done at the wellhead or the base of the wind turbine. But what we really need to know is the energy gain *at the point of use*. For example, while wind turbines can have an EROEI of 20:1 *at the base of the turbine*, the ratio is far lower *at the point of use*, when energy lost in transmission together with the energy cost of balancing intermittency are accounted for. Nevertheless, while there is no agreement on the numbers, the broad point stands – the more energy required to obtain energy, the less energy is available to power the wider economy. This may sound academic, but what it means is that if the EROEI across an economy falls too low, that economy can rapidly enter a "cascading collapse."

The big conceit in economics is that governments and central bankers are in charge. But the economy – the sum total of *everything* we all do – is what physicists call a self-organising dissipative structure. We each interact and transact with individuals and organisations in proximity – physical and virtual – to us, but with little knowledge or understanding of the process beyond that. I flick a switch in my room and the light comes on. And once a quarter I make a payment to an energy supply company for the privilege. But I have no idea where the electricity was generated or whether it was produced using wind, coal, gas or nuclear. If the latter, I have no idea whatsoever where the uranium was mined or how the spent fuel is going to be stored. In the same way, you make a cup of coffee in the morning. You know which shop or supermarket you bought it from, but you may not realise that the brand name is different from the company which supplied it. In any case, it is unlikely you will ever know the name of the agent who arranged the import deal, or the shipping company which brought the coffee to these shores, still less the insurers and bankers whose cover and letters of credit made the transaction possible. It is only when – as happened as a result of the lockdown policies – these long supply chains breakdown that we begin to glimpse the complexity involved.

Behind it all – the very starting point of the economy – is energy. Without food (calories) in our bellies the eight billion humans who collectively perpetuate the economy would slow and eventually die. In the same way, without the fuel to power the vehicles and electricity to run the machines, all economic activity would grind to a halt. In

Steve Keen's words: "Capital without energy is a statue, labour without energy is a corpse."

Within the complex dissipative system that we call the economy though, there are both essential and discretionary activities. The means by which we secure food and clean drinking water are examples of essential activities, while TikTok videos and fashion accessories are discretionary. This becomes more visible during economic downturns when discretionary spending falls as people switch to buying essentials. Less obviously though, apparently discretionary or even frivolous activities are essential to keeping critical functions operating. Roads, for example, are the essential arteries for moving the goods – including food – which keep us alive. But if we were to only allow the movement of essential goods and people to use the roads, we would soon be unable to repair them – whether through road pricing, fuel duties and/or taxation, the revenue from *discretionary* road use allows us to maintain *essential* transport. The same goes for communications. The price of the internet is kept low by all of the annoying cat videos and memes that cause us to waste far too much time. But without them, the advertising model for paying for the internet would fail. Smartphones and laptop computers rely on similar mass use to keep costs down. Each individual unit contains small quantities of metals sourced from around the planet – copper from Chile, gold from South Africa, palladium from Russia, tantalum from Australia, and rare earths from China. This is only economically viable when all of those input costs are shared among billions of consumers.

Without this global interconnectivity and mass consumption, things begin to breakdown. And while there might be sound ecological reasons to support, for example, the post-pandemic decline in new car production – due to a shortage of computer chips – which has forced more drivers to buy second-hand cars, the economic consequences for the employees of car factories are less positive. And if, over time, the lost income and the higher costs cause the cost of motoring to rise, then we may all find ourselves paying higher tax to keep the roads open. It is in this way that problems ripple out across the system. A volcano erupts in Iceland, and the BMW plant in Germany has to close. A Tsunami in Japan brings car production around the world to a temporary halt. A power grid failure in the USA results in chemical plants being closed for a month. In such relatively isolated cases, the system is self-healing – individuals and firms figure out ways of working around the problem. Bigger problems await though, if critical infrastructure itself breaks down.

On 9 August 2019 at 4.53 in the afternoon[6], something *big* struck the British power grid. A massive drop in grid frequency was followed in a matter of seconds by a cascading power outage across southern and eastern England. It didn't help that this occurred at the beginning of Friday's rush hour, causing transport chaos as electric trains came to an abrupt halt and railway signalling stopped working. Road traffic lights failed, causing gridlock as millions of people attempted to get home. Even though power began to be restored within a matter of minutes after heavy industrial consumers had been shut down, transport chaos persisted through the evening.

The immediate cause of the outage was threefold. First, a lightning strike on the Hornsea offshore wind farm tripped its safety system, causing it to disconnect from the grid. Second, a back-up gas generator failed to respond. Third, in response to the sudden loss of power, the grid AI began cutting off power to lower demand. The broader issue though – one which grid engineers have warned about for decades[7] – is that the British grid is overly dependent upon intermittent wind even as back-up generation has been closing – in the case of coal, as a result of government policy. This results in a problem with *inertia*. A large coal or nuclear power station uses heat to turn massive steel turbines. And in the event that heat fluctuates, the inertia in the spinning turbines irons out the moment-to-moment intermittency. Wind turbines have no such means of ironing out intermittency and so, effectively, depend upon other generators' spinning turbines to do the job for them. Which is fine while wind power makes up a small fraction of the energy generated, but when – as in the UK – wind amounts to some 30 percent of electricity, there is a growing risk of too little inertia in the system when one or other generator fails.

This is not just a problem in the UK. The freak winter storm which took out the Texan power grid in February 2021 triggered an almost identical cascading collapse, as the lack of inertia caused the frequency to drop even as back-up generation failed to kick-in in time. The tragic difference was that, whereas Britain's power outage occurred on a balmy August evening, the Texan blackout happened during a severe cold wave, with the result that close to 1,000 people died.

It is not just that the electricity goes off in these crises. A large part of the water and sewage system uses electric pumps so that people's access to drinking water fails almost immediately, and unless the power is restored quickly, sewage begins backing up and overflowing. Most gas central heating systems require an electric connection to operate. And so, a loss of power also means a loss of heating. The fuel pumps at filling stations also require electricity, leaving drivers with just the fuel already in their tanks. Emergency services may have a stock of fuel of their own either to run generators or emergency vehicles, but once exhausted, they are in the same boat as everyone else. Communications cannot be sustained as datacentres and exchanges run out of power. Bank transactions become impossible, and even cash may be difficult to use where retailers depend upon electronic tills. Hospitals face the joint problem of being unable to discharge existing patients and being unable to accept new ones – even those whose conditions are critical. Emergency services can be rapidly overwhelmed both from false alarms when the power goes off – causing fire and burglar alarms to trip – and from the increased demand as the emergency progresses.

Notice, then, that what begins as a failure in one critical infrastructure – in this case the electricity grid – cascades into neighbouring critical infrastructure – water, fuel, healthcare, etc. This is because *all* of our critical infrastructure – effectively our life-support systems – are intimately bound in such a way that a failure in *any* one of them will result in a cascading collapse across all. For example, when protestors blocked the supply of fuel in the UK in September 2000, only the order of collapse was different. Transport was the first to fail. But other systems began to fail as key components, parts, and people were unavailable to maintain them. Hospital operating theatres, for example, came to a standstill due to a growing shortage of suture. The banking crisis in the autumn of 2008 threatened a similar cascade as the ability to transact *globally* almost came to a halt. In a largely electronic monetary system, any loss of the interbank system – whether through a power outage or a credit crunch – would reduce the planet to local bartering within days.

In a world of declining energy and resources, the question is no longer *if* a cascading collapse is going to happen. The question is when? and how bad will it be? In Europe, for example, the technocracy has *chosen* to leave the entire continent starved of fuel due to its refusal to use Russian oil and – particularly – gas. And since gas is the primary back-up fuel to balance the intermittency of wind and solar power, there is a far greater risk of a complete blackout. Indeed, according to Martien Visser, a Lecturer in Energy Transition and Grid Integration at Hanzehogeschool Groningen and Manager of Corporate Strategy at Gasunie, the added complexity in creating an integrated European grid – essential to a transition away from fossil fuels – has made the system *more* vulnerable to a cascading collapse[8]:

"The collective energy interdependency of European countries is increasing even more. Which makes it fairly strange that energy policy is largely a national affair. Needless to say, analyses of the reliability of the energy system are carried out regularly in Brussels. These conclude that the system is in order. But what scenarios are they basing this on? And which political decisions? Was the recent Dutch decision to limit coal use to 25% factored in? What about Belgium, which is threatening to close its nuclear power plants without any adequate replacements? And the new German government, which is likely to accelerate the Kohleausstieg, i.e. the fossil-fuel phase-out. And how about the discussion in the Netherlands concerning the permanent closure of the Groningen system as an emergency reserve for the northwest European gas market?

"Economic theory teaches us that in a free market, supply security is automatically guaranteed. Well, almost always that is, see Texas, among others. The question is whether this economic theory still holds true given the many politically driven decisions. Of course, asking that question effectively answers it. Meanwhile, our society is becoming increasingly dependent on an undisrupted energy supply. While scarcity not only leads to risks to supply security, but also to a sharp increase in energy prices. This is something that we are also seeing right now... continuing on the current path will almost certainly lead to accidents. The question then is not if there will be a European blackout (electricity and/or gas) over the coming years, but when..."

A total blackout sounds bad enough, but the problem doesn't end there. As Christopher Owens, author of *The Blackout Report*[9] explains, the longer the outage lasts, the greater damage to the economy as a whole. And there is no easy fix. In the UK, for example, National Grid – who are likely to be optimistic – anticipate a period of up to a fortnight to restore power after a total shutdown... a so-called "black start." Owens, however, points to a troubling though seldom mentioned problem which might prove to be a show-stopper:

> "A Scottish Black Start Restoration Working Group review of procedures in September 2018 warned that the 2016 closure of Longannet coal-fired power plant in Fife would result in 'severe delays' to the restoration of power north of the border, as it left the gas-fired facility at Peterhead as the only remaining high-power and high-inertia – crucial to stabilise frequency – power station in Scotland...

> "Only a limited number of UK power stations can provide Black Start capacity. Typically, these have tended to be the old-style coal-fired plants equipped with large generators that can produce enough power on-site to restart the facility without the need for any external power... Circumstances aren't helped by the trend towards generation from renewables. For example, most wind farms can't currently Black Start the grid because most depend on some sort of external power before they can start generating. And even though some of the latest designs are now self-starting, they can't yet provide enough reactive power to energise the grid through the long offshore AC cables they connect with."

In other words, having actively closed the coal power stations, failed to invest in replacement nuclear, and willingly disconnected from a large part of the gas supply, Britain – and Europe more broadly – might be unable to restart its electricity grid at all in the aftermath of a complete blackout. In which case, without external aid – which Europe might not be able to supply – we would be looking at a rapid descent into a new dark age... with millions of premature deaths along the way.

For all of the complexity, the issue before us boils down to *energy*. With enough *surplus* energy, we could obtain all of the mineral resources we need via a combination of recycling and sea water filtration. But currently we lack anything like the surplus energy needed to do this... which is why nobody is doing it. Not only do we lack the surplus energy to continue expanding the economy, but we are facing a prolonged period of declining surplus energy. This means that we have a growing list of things that we used to be able to afford but no longer can.

It follows that the simple choice before us is this: we either find a yet-to-be-harnessed energy source which is cheap, abundant and more energy-dense than the fossil fuels we seek to dispense with – and which are depleting anyway – or we begin to de-grow the wider economy in such a way that we maintain as much of our life-support as possible. Neither is particularly easy or even likely. But as the impossibility of business as usual becomes increasingly difficult to ignore and as the impossibility of the various net zero techno-utopias is demonstrated for all to see, the alternative is only chaos and collapse.

Notes

1. 5 June 2019. "Leading scientists set out resource challenge of meeting net zero emissions in the UK by 2050." *Natural History Museum.* https://www.nhm.ac.uk/press-office/press-releases/leading-scientists-set-out-resource-challenge-of-meeting-net-zer.html

2. Michaux, S.P. 2021. *Assessment of the Extra Capacity Required of Alternative Energy Electrical Power Systems to Completely Replace Fossil Fuels.* Geological Survey of Finland

3. Ward JD, Sutton PC, Werner AD, Costanza R, Mohr SH, Simmons CT (2016) Is Decoupling GDP Growth from Environmental Impact Possible? PLoS ONE 11(10): e0164733. https://doi.org/10.1371/journal.pone.0164733

4. Kennedy, P. 2017. *The Rise and Fall of the Great Powers.* William Collins; New Ed edition

5. Shostak, F. 1 May 2017. "Rising Oil Prices Don't Cause Inflation." *Mises Wire.* https://mises.org/wire/rising-oil-prices-dont-cause-inflation

6. Watkins, T. 10 August 2019. "The shape of things to come." *Consciousness of Sheep.* https://consciousnessofsheep.co.uk/2019/08/10/the-shape-of-things-to-come-3/

7. See, for example, the BBC docudrama *"If... The lights go out."* http://news.bbc.co.uk/1/hi/programmes/if/3487048.stm

8. Visser, M. 28 August 2021. "European gas and electricity supply blackouts: The question is not if, but when." *Innovation Origins.* https://innovationorigins.com/en/european-gas-and-electricity-supply-blackouts-the-question-is-not-if-but-when/

9. https://www.theblackoutreport.co.uk/2019/07/04/black-start/

The sum of the parts

During the Brexit referendum campaign, then Prime Minister, David Cameron, visited a car assembly plant on Tyneside, where he was at pains to point out the negative consequences of leaving the EU on the economy. This drew the heckle from one of the factory workers... "Aye, *your* economy." The humour of this aside, it is an example of the common mistake we tend to make in regarding the economy as something separate – indeed, often alien – from us. We imagine it to be something to do with money, stock markets and central banks, and using advanced mathematical modelling which few of us could hope to understand. And in any case, most of us are too busy with the practicalities of putting food on the table to be concerned with such esoteric matters.

Except, of course, that putting food on the table lies at the very heart of the economy. Indeed, the economy encompasses *every* interaction that we have with one another. Even such mundane activities as sharing a meal are a part of the economy – albeit one of a dwindling number which have not been financialised. But that meal required someone having the time to prepare and cook the food. That, in turn, required the relatively complex supply chains which manufacture and distribute cookers, and those which supply the energy to power them. Even more complex supply chains allow food to make its way from the farm to the kitchen – often these days requiring the import of food from around the world which, itself, requires specialised financial arrangements – letters of credit, insurances, etc. – to allow the food to be moved... movement itself depending upon global fleets of ships, aeroplanes and trucks, together with container ports and warehouses, each of which depends upon its own, relatively complex supply chain.

Nor is there a point of origin for these supply chains. Trace any component back far enough, and we arrive at a raw resource which has to be mined, quarried or otherwise obtained from the Earth. The copper wire in a household lighting system, for example, might be traced back to one of the giant open caste copper mines of Chile. But when we get there, we find mining trucks, drilling equipment, explosives, and railway yards, each of which has a supply chain of its own. The mining trucks may have been assembled in Germany or Japan, using components from China and Taiwan, and with minerals from Russia and Australia, and paradoxically, with copper from Chile.

It is often said that the electricity grid is the largest and most complex machine humans have ever created. This though, ignores the global economy itself – this complex web of quadrillions of individual transactions which comprise the web of supply chains which are the sinews of the economy itself. It is what allows you to buy fresh strawberries from a supermarket in Swindon which were picked from a farm outside Santiago just hours ago. It is what permits you to make that purchase with the mere swipe of a plastic card which, through the alchemy of global finance, means that everyone down the line from the haulier and the air freight company to the Chilean farmer gets paid.

The global economy has all of the features of what physicists call a complex dissipative structure. Complex because it has:

- Autonomous agents – the individuals, firms, regulators, governments and international governance bodies which make the whole system work in the way that it does

- Interconnectivity – the system is made up of webs of connections between the autonomous agents

- Interdependence – each agent within the system depends on other agents and the connections between them to continue functioning

- Adaptability – the system is self-organising and in a permanent state of change... there is no steady or "sustainable" state.

The interplay of these features is what makes the system greater than the sum of its parts. That is, no amount of study of the individual parts of the global economy will ever reveal the inner workings of the system as a whole. Moreover, the system is entirely unpredictable. This was Edward Lorenz's "Butterfly Effect" – that even tiny differences in the starting conditions for modelling can result in massive changes to the system as a whole. A butterfly flaps its wings in the Amazon rainforest, setting off a chain of events which lead to a hurricane striking Florida. But a butterfly ten meters away flaps its wings with no discernible effect.

When it comes to the economy, predictability is an even bigger problem because the econometric models used by the economics clerisy are simplified beyond the point of usefulness. They bear no more resemblance to the real world than a child's crayon scribbles. Which is why, time and again, economists claim that "nobody could have seen it coming," when the latest bubble bursts and the new recession breaks over us.

It goes without saying – or at least it should – that anything which is unpredictable is also ungovernable. To a large degree, each of us, operating in our perceived best interests, affects the machine in unpredictable ways, but not often to the point that the system itself is at risk of collapse. Big corporations and governments can have a greater impact on the machine, but consequently the risk of unforeseen negative outcomes is far greater. Most modern politicians exist merely to give psychological reassurance that someone is in charge – an abusive parent, apparently, being better than no parent at all – and generally hope to avoid presiding over a major crisis.

Less obviously, the machine depends upon a growing supply of *exergy* – the proportion of energy available for work – to avoid collapse. As Jim Rickards explains[1]:

> "The more complex, that is dense, the supply chain system, the more energy (including energy in the form of human capital) is required exponentially to keep the system from collapse."

Given the current state of global energy reported in the previous chapter, this suggests that we face an imminent crisis because, while there are still plenty of fossil fuel deposits beneath the ground, the exergy we can derive from them is shrinking as a result of the increased energy cost of recovering them.

At its simplest, the crisis is easy enough to understand. If we used to have 100 units of exergy but now we only have 90, then 10 percent of the things we were doing are going to have to come to an end. The problem with applying this to a system as complex as the economy is that as of 2021, the global economy was powered by 176,431 terawatt hours of energy per year[2] – primarily fossil fuels, hydroelectric and nuclear, with some 5 percent from so-called renewable sources. As the energy available from these sources declines, it is impossible to forecast which economic activities will come to an end nor how this will occur.

This said, it is widely accepted that the wave of populist sentiment which resulted in Britain voting to leave the European Union and in Donald Trump being elected in the USA, was largely driven by an increasingly impoverished precariat living in once booming ex-industrial and small town regions, where the idea of "taking back control" and "making America great again" struck a hopeful chord. Moreover, there is some evidence that those events mark the beginning of the unfolding collapse of global supply chains which has become obvious even to establishment media outlets in the wake of the pandemic lockdowns.

Research by the Centre for Business Prosperity at Aston University[3] found that UK exports to the European Union fell by 22.9% in the first 15 months after the introduction of the EU-UK Trade and Cooperation Agreement, highlighting the disruption to regional supply chains which was already in progress prior to the arrival of SARS-CoV-2. Lori Ann Larocco documents[4] a similar pre-pandemic disruption to global trade resulting from Donald Trump's introduction of trade tariffs and renegotiating of trade agreements beginning in 2017. Both pieces of research are a useful corrective to the establishment media claim that supply chain disruption began with the pandemic – or even more ludicrously with Putin's invasion of Ukraine.

Of course, the insane decision to shut down entire regions of the global economy has served to amplify the supply chain disruptions which were already accelerating. Moreover, the *choice* to engage in an economic war with Russia in response to the invasion of Ukraine has largely backfired on the west because of Russia's role as a major supplier of mineral resources and fossil fuels. Worse still, the *choice* to impound Russia's currency reserves and to steal the assets of oligarchs living in the west has accelerated the global split between the old, western, dollar bloc and an emerging BRICS bloc – the likely result being a major devaluation of the western currencies and a relocalising of the western economies.

It is in this light that we need to view the impossible futures being pursued by the technocracy, with the uncritical backing of a large part of the thwarted – fake left – bourgeoisie. Just as Trump and the Brexiteers' attempts to renegotiate more favourable trade terms sent shockwaves through the global economy, so attempts to force a complex, fossil fuel-powered machine to give up fossil fuels *before* any viable alternative has been found, can only result in a catastrophic collapse of the entire system. Jim Rickards repeats the points made in this book about the nature of technocracy in attempting to explain why so many people seem bent upon suicidal policies[5]:

> "Some scientists who espouse alarmist positions on climate change are in line for large research grants from activist foundations and NGOs. Executives who take alarmist positions may find their stock prices boosted by institutions making ESG-style investments (for environment, social, and governance criteria). Wealth advisers who promote ESG funds profit from management fees and performance fees as the money rolls into those investment schemes. Academics who caution that the climate threat is overblown may be denied tenure or publication and be subject to cancel culture disparagement. Media anchors who promote climate alarmism can improve ratings. Websites that feature climate catastrophe stories get clicks. Politicians can get votes by appearing to 'do something' about a supposed existential threat."

In other words, graft and self-interest amplify long-term climate change and turn it into a fake short-term "climate emergency" which demands radical – and extremely dangerous – action. Which is why, for example, the German government initially regarded the Russian invasion of Ukraine as an opportunity to transition their economy from fossil fuels to some combination of wind, solar and hydrogen. The result being that German industry is in meltdown, ironically with the German wind turbine industry being among the first to close. As Juliet Samuel at the *Telegraph* explains[6]:

"The original error was not with the science of climate change. It was not with the notion that we should phase out coal. But sometime around 2014-16, regulators, lawyers and politicians began to run with the idea that the trashing of 'big oil' (and so on) led by students in feathered war bonnets was costless, popular and green.

"What followed was a co-ordinated effort to run down fossil fuel production, seemingly without a thought for the vastly different environmental impacts of gas versus coal or the need for Western economies and people to enjoy a reliable supply of energy. In 2015, the then Bank of England governor Mark Carney (yes, him again) gave a speech talking up the risk of climate 'stranded assets' – energy investments that would be rendered worthless by climate change legislation…

"Industry saw the writing on the wall. Utilities shut down their long-term gas contracting departments and began to buy gas at the going price on the day, fatally undermining security of supply and making new investment un-financeable. Fossil fuel producers began handing money back to investors. Even state-owned producers, like Qatar, cut investment on the basis that Europe (the UK included) had become an unreliable customer…

"And now? Well, now, as 'big oil' might say: 'We just walked in to find you here with that sad look upon your face.' Europe needs gas. It is pleading for gas. Instead of flying media to gas fields to court capital, the oil and gas men are being flown to the capitals of Europe and begged to invest. Despite the incredible prices, they hesitate.

"The meeting goes like this: 'We need you!' say the politicians. The producers scratch their heads as they mull $20 billion, 20-year investments, and wonder whether, when the war is over and the green bandwagon rolls back into town, the politicians will still sound so sweet on them. 'Your green targets still say we need to shut down by 2030,' they point out. To which Europe says: 'Well, of course. Fossil fuels are evil!'"

To be clear, for self-interested reasons – the preservation of its own wealth and power – but under the guise of concern about trade, public health and environmental issues, the technocracy has thrown policy hand grenades into the complex global machinery of a global economy which is as much to do with providing our life support as it is with money and frivolous consumption. What we are currently experiencing in the shape of economic disruption and shortages is the system attempting to rebalance at a lower energetic level. But this may not be possible. The shocks that have been inflicted may have already fatally wounded industrial civilisation itself. Even Rickards – ultimately an optimist and possibly reflecting more sober views within the US establishment – envisages a process of stabilisation taking several decades[7]:

> "The point of this expansive list of supply chain impediments is that none are going away soon. Climate change alarm is an effective channel for globalist ambitions in the financial sector. It will not fade quickly, even as its unfounded claims are increasingly disproved. Energy shortages and higher energy prices go hand in hand with the elites' green agenda promulgated from the bastions of academia, government, and banks. This damage will last for years. The turning point may not occur until elites themselves are freezing in the dark. China's conscious decoupling from existing supply chains is part of a broader strategy of self-reliance driven by Xi Jinping's insecure standing and a candid acknowledgment that the West is decoupling from China in any case. Chinese decoupling will take decades unless interrupted by regime change, which will be even more disruptive. In the West, onshoring and reshoring to

democratic locales as advocated by the Five Eyes is under way yet will also take decades."

It is possible that a process of disintegration and de-growth will allow western states to recreate some of the – far less complex – national economies of an earlier age. Industrial processes which were so casually closed or offshored may be rebuilt. Consumption and energy use may fall back to levels last seen half a century or more ago. And would that be such a bad thing? Those of us who grew up in the 1960s do not remember it as a particularly deprived era. And while such a lifestyle would involve foregoing many of the things we currently take for granted – the internet, GPS, chemotherapy, global food supplies, private cars, microwave ovens, colour TV, etc. – the re-emergence of non-financialised family and friendship ties and activities would surely make for a healthier way of life.

The trouble is that complexity doesn't really work that way. In a talk at a FEASTA conference in 2011[8], David Korowicz made the point using a thought experiment. Suppose all of the computer chips manufactured in the past 20 years were to stop working. Does that mean that we would revert to the economy and way of life of 2003? Not at all, because our complex self-organising system is primed for efficiency rather than resilience. As a consequence, we do not maintain old goods and infrastructure just in case something breaks. A failure of twenty years' worth of computer chips would likely leave us digging up landfill tips in a desperate attempt to recover older chips... and even then, we would struggle to maintain just a tiny fraction of the computerised infrastructure of the modern world.

Okay, barring another Carrington Event[9], it is unlikely that all of the chips are going to fail at the same time. But this may not be enough to save us if we are hit with a truly global crisis such as the threatened collapse of international banking in 2008. Korowicz's argument is that because of the interconnected nature of the economy, a failure in any one of our critical infrastructures would quickly cascade to infect all of the others. Moreover, because the economy has reached a level of complexity far beyond anyone's ability to control, the risk of a cascading collapse has grown with each passing year.

Rickards is undoubtedly correct in setting out a need to simplify and de-grow. But it is far from clear that there is a path to achieving this which doesn't risk triggering the very cascading collapse that we ideally wish to avoid. And if such a cascade is triggered, there is no safety net in the form of older, perhaps steam-powered, technologies still less the horses needed to revert to the pre-industrial conditions of the early eighteenth century. The unimaginable – but real – danger is that by undermining critical infrastructure we may inadvertently plunge ourselves into a new dark age.

It is for this reason that I refer to the modern technocracy – and the fake left which rallies behind its cause – as a Death Cult. Because they are unconcerned about – and likely oblivious to – the fragility of the complex global economy and the billions of people who depend upon it. Far from seeking to gradually reform the machine, their starting point is a perceived need to destroy it... to raise it to the ground so that the techno-utopian alternative can grow in its place. Except, of course, that is not what happens when you disintegrate complex precision machinery. Throwing spanners into the engines of precision racing cars seldom causes them to go faster, and more often results in their breaking beyond repair. The same is true of imposing bans on fossil fuels before viable alternatives have been invented, disconnecting entire continents from energy and mineral resources in the vain hope of forcing regime change in Russia, imposing ESG investment rules on an already over-indebted financial system, or even simply turning a blind-eye to economic crises which you – probably wrongly

– hope will create the conditions to impose digital currencies for which you lack the energy to operate.

This is hardly the "conspiracy theory" that so many people believe some "they" are fomenting. The technocracy is all too open about its view of the future. For example, as Thomas Fazi points out[10], the World Economic Forum has set out its anti-democratic vision to be imposed upon the rest of us:

> "In its own words, the WEF's project is 'to redefine the international system as constituting a wider, multifaceted system of global cooperation in which intergovernmental legal frameworks and institutions are embedded as a core, but not the sole and sometimes not the most crucial, component'.
>
> "While this may sound fairly benign, it neatly encapsulates the basic philosophy of globalism: insulating policy from democracy by transferring the decision-making process from the national and international level, where citizens theoretically are able to exercise some degree of influence over policy, to the supranational level, by placing a self-selected group of unelected, unaccountable 'stakeholders' — mainly corporations — in charge of global decisions concerning everything from energy and food production to the media and public health. The underlying undemocratic philosophy is the same one underpinning the philanthrocapitalist approach of people such as Bill Gates, himself a long-time partner of the WEF: that non-governmental social and business organisations are best suited to solve the world's problems than governments and multilateral institutions."

Nor does the WEF make any secret of which interests it really serves:

"Even though the WEF has increasingly focused its agenda on fashionable topics such as environmental protection and social entrepreneurship, there is little doubt as to which interests Schwab's brainchild is actually promoting and empowering: the WEF is itself mostly funded by around 1,000 member companies — typically global enterprises with multi-billion dollar turnovers, which include some of the world's biggest corporations in oil (Saudi Aramco, Shell, Chevron, BP), food (Unilever, The Coca-Cola Company, Nestlé), technology (Facebook, Google, Amazon, Microsoft, Apple) and pharmaceuticals (AstraZeneca, Pfizer, Moderna). The composition of the WEF's board is also very revealing, including Laurence D. Fink, CEO of Blackrock, David M. Rubenstein, co-chairman of the Carlyle Group, and Mark Schneider, CEO of Nestlé. There's no need to resort to conspiracy theories to posit that the WEF's agenda is much more likely to be tailored to suit the interests of its funders and board members — the world's ultra-wealthy and corporate elites — rather than to 'improving the state of the world', as the organisation claims."

Like communism and the Green New Deal, so long as the policies dreamed up by the technocracy remain as no more than discussion items at an elitist conference where delegates notoriously fail to practice what they preach, then nobody is harmed. Unfortunately, having infiltrated governments across the world via the Global Young Leaders program, the technocracy has begun enacting its policies for real... with predictably negative results. This was most starkly demonstrated in Sri Lanka last summer[11], after an already highly unstable state attempted to turn WEF fantasy economics into real life:

"Sri Lanka was supposed to be the poster child for the Great Green New Reset, scoring a 98 percent ESG (Environment, Social and Governance) ranking. Sri

Lankan President Gotabaya Rajapaksa winning considerable praise from globalist leaders and climate activists alike for his speech to the COP26 conference in Glasgow last November...

"In spite of praise from organisations like the WEF and the world bank, however, the Sri Lankan economy was highly indebted and vulnerable to economic shocks long before the country's leaders decided that a mass crash diet was in order. The country's main sources of foreign currency – without which it could not repay its debts – are tea exports and tourism. Tourism was, of course, crushed in 2020 and 2021, as countries locked down and air travel ground to a halt. In 2022, moreover, air travel is still disrupted, and far fewer consumers can afford international travel.

"Meanwhile, despite the Sri Lankan government believing that the switch to niche organic tea exports would make up in foreign currency for the loss of yield, the reality is that the market for organic tea is miniscule. With a generalised increase in prices around the world eating into consumer spending, lower cost has become more important than environmental status for most consumers. The result being that Sri Lanka's income from tea exports has crashed.

"The fertiliser ban, which has resulted in mass hunger, was merely the final act of a national government in thrall to an intellectually bankrupt global technocracy whose prescriptions for prosperity break all of the laws of thermodynamics. As they flee the country in fear of their lives, they may contemplate the one common feature of all social revolutions... bellies rumbling with hunger."

This, of course, is the same economic collapse and widespread hunger that the technocracy would like to impose on the wider world. Not out of some heinous plan to depopulate the planet – a process which is already well underway as it happens, simply because birth rates are collapsing even as peak life expectancy is disappearing in the rear-view mirror – but simply because their attempt to address the bottleneck of crises *while maintaining their own wealth and power* is doomed to fail. But in proving this point, a lot of people across the world are going to starve to death.

Whether it is the World Economic Forum, the European Commission, the World Health Organisation, the International Monetary Fund, The Bank of England, the Adam Smith Institute, the CBI, the TUC, the BBC, or any of the other millions of technocratic organisations with acronyms which consistently get things wrong, no matter how benign the intention, tyranny it remains. As Saunders Lewis[12] put it:

> "Of all tyrannies, a tyranny sincerely exercised for the good of its victims may be the most oppressive. It would be better to live under robber barons than under omnipotent moral busybodies. The robber baron's cruelty may sometimes sleep, his cupidity may at some point be satiated; but those who torment us for our own good will torment us without end for they do so with the approval of their own conscience."

In its supreme piety, our technocracy, increasingly ungrounded from and resentful of planet Earth itself, has chosen to awaken and set in motion a storm greater than it could ever have imagined... we will all pay the price of their folly.

Notes

1. Rickards, James. Sold Out (p. 58). Penguin Books Ltd. Kindle Edition

2. Ritchie, H. Roser, M. and Rosado, P. 2022. "Energy". Published online at *OurWorldInData.org*. https://ourworldindata.org/energy

3. Du, J., E.B. Satoglu and Shepotylo, O. November 2022. *Post-Brexit UK Trade: An Update.* www.lbpresearch.ac.uk/wp-content/uploads/2022/11/Post-Brexit-UK-Trade-Updated.pdf

4. Larocco, L.A. 2019. *Trade War: Containers Don't Lie, Navigating the Bluster.* Marine Money, Inc

5. Rickards, James. Sold Out (pp. 91-92). Penguin Books Ltd. Kindle Edition

6. Samuel, J. 26 August 2022. "How governments and the cult of net zero wrecked the energy market." *Telegraph.* www.telegraph.co.uk/news/2022/08/26/how-governments-cult-net-zero-wrecked-energy-market/

7. Rickards, James. Ibid.

8. Korowicz, D. 2011. *The Modern Economy, Civilisation, Complexity and Collapse.* https://youtu.be/Lqaw2fix3q0

9. The 1859 solar flare event which resulted in an electromagnetic pulse affecting the world's – fortunately few – electronic devices. See, e.g., Choi, C.Q. 7 September 2022. "What if the Carrington Event, the largest solar storm ever recorded, happened today?" *Live Science.* www.livescience.com/carrington-event

10. Fazi, T. 16 January 2023. "How the Davos elite took back control." *UnHerd.*

https://unherd.com/2023/01/how-the-davos-elite-took-back-control/

11. Watkins, T. 14 July 2022. "The great unravelling." *Consciousness of Sheep*. https://consciousnessofsheep.co.uk/2022/07/14/the-great-unravelling

12. Lewis, C.S. 1971. *God in the Dock: Essays on Theology and Ethics*

Earthbound

"In my work with the defendants [at the Nuremberg Trials 1945-1949] I was searching for the nature of evil and I now think I have come close to defining it. A lack of empathy. It's the one characteristic that connects all the defendants, a genuine incapacity to feel with their fellow men... Evil, I think, is the absence of empathy."

– Captain G. M. Gilbert, US Army psychologist

The purpose of the technocracy is power. Not, as their propaganda has it, power for some noble purpose like reversing climate change or improving the lot of the oppressed. But power for its own sake. This, perhaps, is the biggest mistake made by the fake left, who see in the propaganda a shared interest in bringing an end to the last remnants of democracy and assume that they will be the inheritors of the revolution that follows. But the technocracy does not want their agreement, merely their compliance. And when the time comes, as has happened in every previous revolution, the proposed new order will eat its own children first... useful idiots indeed!

Ignore their words, and look at their deeds, and the most obvious thing about the technocracy is their contempt for their fellow humans. How else are we to judge people who accumulate enormous wealth but fail to use even a tiny fraction of it for the public good? How else are we to judge people who talk about locking millions in so-called "15-minute cities" to cut carbon emissions, while they fly around the world in carbon-spewing private jets? How else are we to judge those who claim that within the decade the seas will rise to engulf our cities, before buying themselves luxury mansions on the Californian coast? And, how else should we judge those who feast on prime beef, while telling the rest of us we will have to eat insects?

It is this lack of empathy for the condition of billions of ordinary people which marks our technocracy as uniquely evil... even if its graft is only beginning to produce mass deaths. It is not though, just humanity that the technocracy is determined to stand above and apart from. Its far greater hubris comes in its attempt to stand above and beyond Planet Earth itself. We get a hint of this in the shape of the latest vegan eggs. Not just a vegan binding agent to replace eggs in plant-based cooking. But actual eggs, with whites and yolks and plastic shells. Vegan eggs which look, feel and taste just like the real thing. Superficially, it doesn't really matter. If vegans wish to replicate the animal products they eschew, that's up to them. Although personally, I might be more attracted to an entirely new range of plant-based products, different in taste and texture to anything encountered previously. After all, who isn't in favour of diversity? There is more to this than meets the eye though. It points to a common desire among the so-called Virtuals/Anywheres largely found among the technocracy not just to exercise control over the world, but to actually *replace* planet Earth with a counterfeit alternative. It is not enough, for example, simply to cease exploiting animals, we must eradicate the animals and replace them with a virtual alternative. This, perhaps, is why climate change has emerged as the only one of myriad bottleneck crises that the technocracy permits us to discuss, since it is the one which most readily lends itself to the replacement of that which is real with an ersatz techno-utopian alternative under technocratic control.

In a similar vein, we find a paper[1] by Martha C. Nussbaum, a Professor of Law and Ethics at the University of Chicago, which made the case that wild animals should be prevented from killing and eating each other:

> "All land in our world is thoroughly under human control. Thus 'wild animals' in Africa live on animal refuges maintained by the governments of various

nations, which control admission to them, defend them from poachers (only sometimes successfully), and support the lives of animals in them through a range of strategies (including spraying for tsetse flies and many other matters). There would be no rhinos or elephants left in the world if humans did not intervene."

This, reasonably enough, has been dismissed as an example of the, sadly all too common, "woke" nonsense which emanates from western universities these days. However, from an ethical standpoint, more thoughtful critics have challenged the view that humans have some moral responsibility for regulating the behaviours of other species. Meanwhile, those with a background in ecology point to the dangerous unforeseen consequences which can result from interfering with the predator-prey relationships within something as complex as an ecosystem. The biggest problem of all though – at least from the perspective set out in this book – is in that first statement... that "all land in our world is thoroughly under human control." From a legal starting point, perhaps "control" is equated with some form of property ownership. But legal ownership is only really a claim to be able to do certain things with or to a piece of land. At a small scale, you might have a right to engage in any legally approved activity in the garden of your house – to play games, enjoy al fresco meals, or to grow food, for example. But this is very different to the claim that your garden is *thoroughly* under your *control*. Sure, you might cut back weeds or use pest control to prevent rodents entering your house. But you can do little to stop a passing hawk from swooping in to take one of those rodents for itself, still less prevent spiders from eating flies or nematodes eating slugs. Indeed – as my son and his partner know all too well, even if you feed your domestic cat with the best food available – you would have to be a miracle worker to prevent them bringing in birds, mice and other small creatures... only a fraction of which survive to be put back. It should go without saying that attempting to regulate animal behaviour in a far less cultivated setting is a non-starter.

There is something deeper going on here though. Clearly, Nussbaum is wildly overestimating both humanity's separation from the ecosystem as well as the true extent to which humans can exercise control. In this, Nussbaum is doing no more than reflecting the hubris of her class – technocratic and virtual. Regulating animal behaviour is surely no more techno-utopian than imagining that we might run our complex global economy on a fraction of the energy it currently consumes and using energy sources which are largely unfit for purpose. Nevertheless, the technocracy has brought us to the brink of economic collapse in pursuit of precisely that utopian fantasy.

Just as the technocracy had to pretend that the western states had become meritocracies in order to maintain that their privilege was earned solely by their own efforts, so they have had to pretend that they have near total control of the world in order to mask their impotence. Nobody seriously believes that Nussbaum's paper is going to launch a new crusade to stop cheetahs eating antelopes or crocodiles from ripping the limbs off zebras. The point of the paper is primarily to bolster the technocracy's self-image as the masters of the world they seek to rule... a secondary purpose, presumably, being to accuse poorly paid farmers and game park workers of being animal abusers for failing to prevent the carnage.

Control, of course, is precisely what humans have been trying to do even before we became homo sapiens[2]. The strength and curse of humanity is that somewhere in our evolutionary past, we outsourced a part of our digestive system. This is evident in our small jaws and teeth, weak jaw muscles, and our shortened digestive tract – all of which are the product of our use of cooking to, in effect, pre-digest the food we eat. The massive advantage this conferred upon us was that, unlike most predators, we didn't need to sleep for hours while we digested our food. This, in turn, gave us more time to think about and to act upon the world around us. This then allowed us to create the first rudimentary technologies.

It is essential that we understand what technology truly is. From the very start, technology was about harnessing *energy*. And while this might be beneficial to apes which have learned to poke sticks into termite nests, or birds which have learned to place nuts under the wheels of passing cars, it was far more visceral to human animals which rely upon cooked food and *depend* upon fire to pre-digest it for us. From hot stones thrown into pots of water to boil plants, to flint spearheads to allow more effective hunting, the aim was always to allow us to put less energy in, in order to get more energy out.

Although far more complex, we continue to do the same thing with the modern global economy. Most of our technologies being either energy-harvesting or energy-saving – although the more affluent we have become, i.e., the more *surplus* energy we enjoy, the more we have been able to develop technologies which temporarily satisfy the dopamine (pleasure-seeking/pain-avoiding) system... the screens which virtuals spend most of their time behind being one of the most pervasive of these. Productivity – something that economists, politicians and central bankers are increasingly concerned about these days – is merely a posh term for energy efficiency, i.e., using technology to do more with less energy.

The story which the technocracy has told us – and which, very likely, most of us still believe – is of the upward arc of human progress, as measured by technological development. As we have seen though, disruptive science and the technological patents based upon it, has been in decline for decades. And as physicist Tom Murphy has pointed out[3], there is little in today's technology that would not have been understood by our great grandparents:

> "Imagine magically transporting a person through time from 1885 into 1950—as if by a long sleep—and also popping a 1950 inhabitant into today's world... Which one has a more difficult time making sense of the updated world around them? Which one sees more 'magic,' and which one has more familiar points of reference?
>
> "Our 19th Century rube would fail to recognize cars/trucks, airplanes, helicopters, and rockets; radio, and television (the telephone was 1875, so just missed this one); toasters, blenders, and electric ranges. Also unknown to the world of 1885 are inventions like radar, nuclear fission, and atomic bombs. The list could go on. Daily life would have undergone so many changes that the old timer would be pretty bewildered, I imagine... The list of 'magic' devices would seem to be innumerable.
>
> "Now consider what's unfamiliar to the 1950 sleeper. Look around your environment and imagine your life as seen through the eyes of a mid-century dweller. What's new? Most things our eyes land on will be pretty well understood. The big differences are cell phones (which they will understand to be a sort of telephone, albeit with no cord and capable of sending telegram-like communications, but still figuring that it works via radio waves rather than magic), computers (which they will see as interactive televisions), and GPS navigation (okay: that one's thought to be magic even by today's folk). They will no doubt be impressed with miniaturization as an evolutionary spectacle, but will tend to have a context for the functional capabilities of our gizmos.
>
> "Telling ourselves that the pace of technological transformation is ever-increasing is just a fun story we

like to believe is true. For many of us, I suspect, our whole world order is built on this premise."

It is two decades since the last passenger boarded a supersonic commercial flight. Indeed, most air travel takes longer today than it did two decades ago because the need for fuel efficiency is now far greater than speed. This though, is just one high profile activity of a growing list of things we used to be able to do but no longer can. Consider, for example, the once ubiquitous automated car wash, now largely replaced not by some even funkier AI controlled robotics, but by the hands of migrant workers paid, one suspects, a lot less than the minimum wage. Two processes are at work here. First, energy itself is getting harder to obtain. History is littered with civilisations which collapsed after they burned through their stock of trees. Ours was different because we stumbled upon stores of fossilised solar energy, first in the form of coal, and later oil and gas. As Nobel Prize-winning chemist Frederick Soddy[4] observed in the 1930s:

> "All the requirements of pre-scientific men were met out of the solar energy of their own times. The food they ate, the clothes they wore, and the wood they burnt could be envisaged, as regards the energy content which gives them use-value, as stores of sunlight. But in burning coal one releases a store of sunshine that reached the earth millions of years ago. In so far as it can be used for the purposes of life, the scale of living may be, to almost any necessary extent, augmented...
>
> "The flamboyant era through which we have been passing is due not to our own merits, but to our having inherited accumulations of solar energy from the carboniferous era, so that life for once has been able to live beyond its income. Had it but known it, it might have been a merrier age!"

The second process is a little more obscure. Once humans learn to harness energy for a particular purpose, it is normally followed by a process of making efficiency gains. As a popular social media meme points out, there were just 66 years between the Wright Flyer's maiden flight and Neil Armstrong setting foot on the Moon. This is meant to imply an exponential development of technology. But that's not really how it works. Rather, technology follows an "S" curve of diminishing returns:

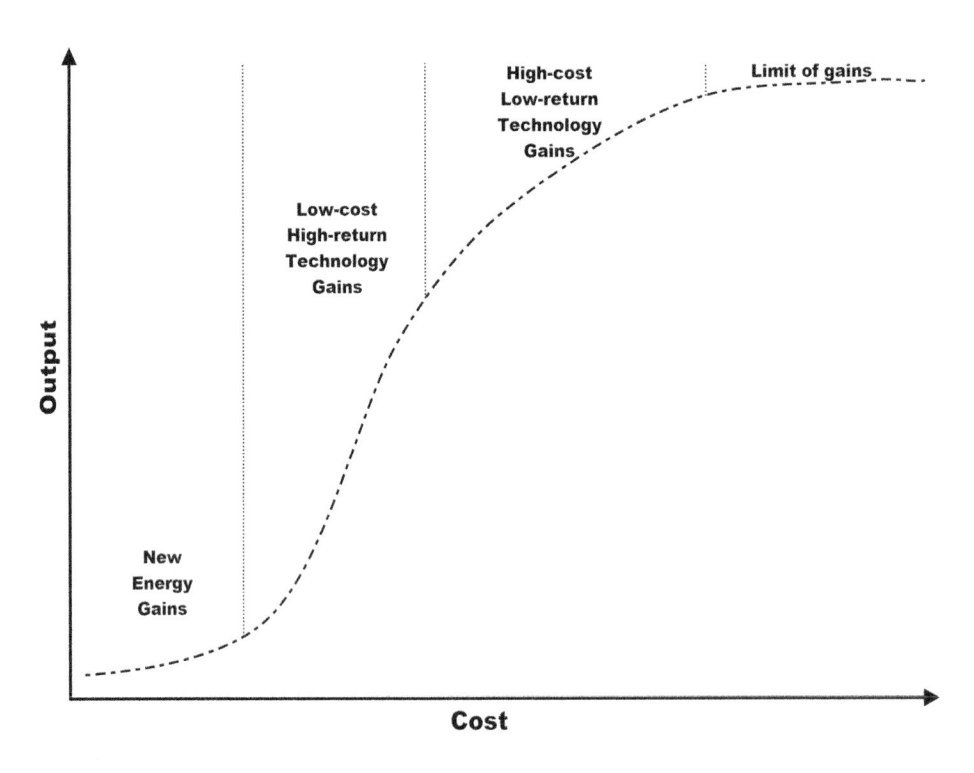

At its simplest, this is the Second Law of Thermodynamics in action. That is, that in any process energy is always lost as waste heat. With most prototype technologies, the waste heat is massive, with only a tiny fraction of the energy captured for useful work – *exergy*. Usually though, relatively cheap and easy productivity improvements may be made to dramatically increase the exergy. However, the thermodynamic limit remains, and the closer we get to it, the harder and more expensive the productivity gains become. Indeed, in the human economy – because we use money as a not entirely reliable proxy for exergy – we often end up subsidising a technology with exergy from elsewhere.

Consider, for example, the development of railways in Britain. Trevithick's 1804 steam locomotive managed to haul a load of iron from the iron works at Merthyr down the Taff Valley to the canal quay at Abercynon at about 15 miles per hour, before having to be pulled back up the valley with horses. And yet, within a few years, easy upgrades such as improved sleepers and bevelled wheels increased the speed and durability to the point that Britain enjoyed its first railway boom. By the end of the century, rail travel was commonplace, with the network of branch lines extending into sleepy villages all over England and Wales. Improvements continued through the interwar years until, in 1938, the Pacific Class *Mallard* set the world steam locomotive speed record of 126 miles per hour. And here's the thing, that record has stood to the present day. Not, I suspect, that with enough money and resources, someone couldn't beat it. But because *Mallard* needed huge state subsidies to operate services which few tax-payers could afford to use. That is, it had reached an *economic* limit of productivity gains.

The common objection to raising economic limits is that, "they can always find money to fight wars." Indeed, giving voice to techno-utopian fantasy, George Monbiot[5] is not the first, and probably won't be the last climate activist to call for a war-like response:

> "The astonishing story of how the US entered the second world war should be on everyone's minds as Cop26 approaches... So what stops the world from responding with the same decisive force to the greatest crisis humanity has ever faced? It's not a lack of money or capacity or technology. If anything, digitisation would

make such a transformation quicker and easier. It's a problem that Roosevelt faced until Pearl Harbor: a lack of political will. Now, just as then, public hostility and indifference, encouraged by legacy industries (today, above all, fossil fuel, transport, infrastructure, meat and media), outweighs the demand for intervention...

"As the US mobilisation showed, when governments and societies decide to be competent, they can achieve things that at other times are considered impossible. Catastrophe is not a matter of fate. It's a matter of choice."

Overlooked, however, is that when Japan bombed Pearl Harbor, almost all of the oil was still in the ground. Indeed, 90 percent of the oil humans have burned has been consumed in the decades since 1945... 50 percent of it since 1990. As Professor of Petroleum and Chemical Engineering, Tad Patzek retorts[6]:

"To compare the WWII industrial effort with the global dislocation necessary to ameliorate some of the effects of climate change is surprisingly naive... This comparison also neglects to account for the human population that has almost quadrupled between the 1940s and now, and the resource consumption that has increased almost 10-fold. The world today cannot grow its industrial production the way we did during WWII. There is simply not enough of the planet Earth left to be devoured."

As people across the western states have been discovering to their cost in recent months, if something is in short supply, simply printing currency to pay for it results only in rising prices. And this is all that would happen in the event that countries attempted a New Deal or War mobilisation to address climate change *without* some new, and yet-to-be-discovered energy source, or – in the case of nuclear power – an appropriate technology to harness it. But as with Nussbaum's paper, that's not really the point.

The aim of the technocracy is not to actually *do something* about climate change – or, indeed, any of the myriad bottleneck crises breaking over us – but to pretend firstly, that they are in control, secondly that their utopian response is feasible, we just need to give it time, and thirdly to stigmatise the rest of us as "climate deniers" for continuing to need to travel to work or for wanting our homes not to be freezing.

That is the broad point of this book. That the particular iteration of corporatism – neoliberal technocracy – that has arisen across the western states in the last couple of decades is a product of a decades long economic decline which, itself, is the result of an energetic decline. In many ways, the corruption and failure which has become so obvious in an age of social media and instant rebuttal, was always there. What has changed is the economic basis for the stealth usurpation of democracy. Like the people of communist China, in the wake of the crises of the 1970s, western populations entered into a Faustian pact with the technocrats through which we allowed democracy to be weakened and undermined in exchange for growing economic prosperity. And even after the rot had set in, the financial alchemy practiced by the banking and finance technocrats allowed us to enjoy one final debt-based blow-out before the party came to an end.

Just at the point when the technocracy has brought human civilisation to the brink of an economic, energetic, and environmental collapse, they have begun to appear less confident. They are like the stage magician who has borrowed your watch, wrapped it in a handkerchief, and smashed it to smithereens, only for an expression of confusion to cross his face… he never did learn the second part of the trick, where he was supposed to give your watch back in even better order than it was before. It is increasingly obvious that the technocratic trick of "Building Back Better" is looking a lot closer to John Michael Greer's[7] "collapse now and avoid the rush!" And so, the technocracy reaches for ever more authoritarian measures to silence anybody on the outside of the invisible technocratic walls from pointing out, as it were, that the emperor has no clothes. Their one claim to legitimacy – that they could make the world better for everyone – turned out to be a lie. The utopia that they promised was just around the corner turned out to be a mirage. Across the western world, all of the measures of improvement – life expectancy, prosperity, wellbeing, etc. have gone into reverse. And the very thing which they told us made western societies great in the first place – that we conducted research for ourselves and were open to changing our minds when the facts contradicted the narrative – are now verboten – subject to an increasingly intolerant "cancel culture," which stymies precisely the kind of disruptive scientific inquiry and debate that is essential to any possibility of providing humanity with a route through the bottleneck without inflicting a mass die off on an unprecedented scale.

It is for this reason that I refer to the technocracy and its fake left supporters as a Death Cult. Not only because they ignore and censor discussion of almost all of the bottleneck crises save for the one from which they can still extract profit. But also, because their demand that we funnel the final energy, resources and research effort into a techno-utopian non-solution which demonstrably lacks any grounding in reality, has deprived us of any real chance of taking an alternative course which might at least have spared billions of people the premature death that now looks likely.

The urgency of the task before us cannot be overstated, since the bottleneck crises threaten our life support systems. And none of us in the developed and even the developing states is prepared for the horrors that would entail. Elsewhere[8], I coined the idea of a "Brown New Deal," which recognises not just that we need to end fossil fuel use because of the environmental impacts, but also because we have already passed the thermodynamic peak of fossil fuel extraction – Mother Earth's way of forcing us to change our ways.

It has been said that our biggest problem is over-population. And there is much to this within the current system. Too many humans are consuming too much of what remains of Planet Earth to be sustainable. Less often explained though, is that almost all of the humans who are over-consuming live in the developed western states, particularly the USA where, until recently, some five percent of the world's population have happily consumed a quarter of the world's resources. Even less often noted, of course, is that the very technocracy which spends much of its time telling the rest of us to tighten our belts, is responsible for consuming the most resources of all. Indeed, if the technocracy were to voluntarily agree to a lifestyle equivalent to that of someone on welfare benefits in the western states, this would be enough to stave off concerns about overshoot.

This is another way of pointing out that the problem is not really about population. the real problem is with consumption. And this, in turn, is a matter of energy. With sufficient *surplus* energy (far more than we currently have) for example, we might operate the carbon capture and storage technologies which are currently too (energy) expensive to operate. A similar energy surplus might allow us to filter all of the raw materials we need from sea water – perhaps producing clean drinking water as a by-product. With sufficient surplus energy we might sustain a population even greater than the eight billion of us currently residing on Planet Earth.

The problem though, is that no such surplus energy exists. Indeed, perhaps the greatest of the bottleneck crises – because it removes our ability to respond to the rest – is that our surplus energy has been in decline since the 1970s – precisely the point at which technological progress went into reverse. The neoliberal revolution, which allowed the technocracy to usurp democracy, was a temporary fix, via the ruthless pursuit of (energy) efficiency at the expense of resilience and, indeed, of future energy security. Other pathways were available – although the number and scope is declining fast – but these would have involved the technocracy foregoing its wealth and power, and so they were never entertained.

Chemical energy – in practice, breaking the bonds of the electrons surrounding atoms – reached its high point with oil-based fuels and the development of the internal combustion engine. Neither solar panels nor wind turbines can provide more than a fraction of the exergy we derive from oil. Moreover, because the renewable energy they harvest comes to us in the form of electricity, it is impractical for use in industrial heating and most heavy transportation. Only breaking the bonds within the nucleus of atoms offers the *theoretical* means of accessing an even more energy-dense source of exergy than fossil fuels. But the problem with this is that we are largely clueless as to how this might be achieved.

Splitting atoms is simple enough, it happens day-in and day-out within hundreds of nuclear reactors around the world. The problem is that these reactors have been connected to incredibly expensive nineteenth century steam turbines. And while that is great for replacing coal in electricity generation, it is nowhere close to providing the surplus energy that would be needed to allow us to cease using fossil fuels while maintaining – and possibly even growing – our complex global economy. Moreover, nuclear power comes with a host of public relations problems of its own.

This said, some kind of disruptive scientific and engineering breakthrough in nuclear power is currently the only way in which humanity gets to come through the bottleneck with our industrial civilisation intact. This would give rise to problems of its own, of course – just as the oil age created problems which would have been inconceivable to nineteenth century coal age dwellers. Nevertheless, insofar as we are likely to have a lot of physicists and engineers with more time on their hands as declining surplus energy causes the economy to shrink, then using what remains of governments' ability to make research grants, then focusing on some "out of the box" research into what we might be able to do with the energy in the nucleus of atoms – other than operating multi-billion dollar pressure cookers – is far more useful than messing around with that other nineteenth century technology, the battery.

In the meantime, the rest of us need to plan for the worse. Not least because there is something like a 99.9 percent likelihood that attempts to develop nuclear power to the point that it can replace fossil fuels are going to fail. What this means is that the populations of the western states are going to have to adapt to a far more materially and energetically simpler way of life. If you want to see a real-life version of what we might expect if this is handled badly, take a look at the various tent shanties which have been growing like mushrooms in the poorer districts of most western cities. Look also at the burgeoning rates of violent and acquisitive crime and, indeed, at the inability of police forces to deal with it. Insofar as an alternative presents itself, perhaps post-Soviet Cuba offers the best hope. That country survived oil starvation following the collapse of the Soviet Union by permitting and encouraging the people to grow food on any patch of land that was uncultivated, irrespective of who claimed to own the land. In other words, by putting our efforts into maintaining essentials like food and clean drinking water, and by working collectively to optimise our efforts, we might just get through.

Powering down is unlikely to be pleasant, but properly managed it is far preferable to a complete and rapid collapse. Dwindling surplus energy dictates that we will do it one way or the other. This is where the Brown New Deal comes in – we need to use the remaining *accessible* fossil fuels both to power down and to conduct the research into more energy-dense alternatives, so that, in the event that the research fails to pay off, we will still have a tolerable economy as the surplus energy disappears.

In any case, so long as the technocracy is left to rule – and there are few democratic institutions left to return it to its proper, subservient, position – the only future open to us is the final accumulation of wealth – hiding behind the graft of ESG investing and various versions of net zero – while the economies of the world are plunged into a final, fatal, collapse from which there will be no coming back. In this, perhaps, there is still a chance that at least some within the technocracy will wake up to that other truth about collapse and revolution – not only does the revolution eat its children, it also decapitates the elites.

There is an easy – but fatal – alternative too. We might continue with our passivity in the face of global technocratic institutions which appear all powerful. The technocracy, in turn, can continue virtue signalling even as its actions – or, more correctly, lack thereof – betray its words. And we may all, and without reason, continue to trust the technocracy when they tell us that the promised techno-utopia will be putting in an appearance any day now... we just need to be patient. That is, we can continue to devour what remains of planet Earth in our debt-based throwaway landfill economy until such time as ever deeper bottleneck economic, energetic and environmental crises overwhelm us...

Après ça, le déluge.

Notes

1. Nussbaum, M.C. 8 December 2022. "A Peopled Wilderness." *The New York Review.* https://www.nybooks.com/articles/2022/12/08/a-peopled-wilderness-martha-c-nussbaum

2. For a deeper discussion of this issue see: Watkins, T. 2020. *Why Don't Lions Chase Mice?: An introduction to energy-based economics*

3. Murphy, T. 16 September 2015. "You Call this Progress?" *Do The Math.* https://dothemath.ucsd.edu/2015/09/you-call-this-progress

4. Soddy, F. 1932. *Wealth and Debt*

5. Monbiot, G. 20 October 2021. "Think big on climate: the transformation of society in months has been done before." *Guardian.* https://www.theguardian.com/commentisfree/2021/oct/20/us-war-footing-1941-climate-emergency-earth-pearl-harbor?

6. Patzek, T. 13 October 2018. "All is well on our planet Earth, isn't it?" *Life Itself.* https://patzek-lifeitself.blogspot.com/2018/10/all-is-well-on-our-planet-earth-isnt-it.html

7. Greer, J.M. 2015. *Collapse Now and Avoid the Rush: The Best of The Archdruid Report.* Founders House Publishing.

8. Watkins, T. 4 June 2020. "A Brown New Deal." *Consciousness of Sheep.* https://consciousnessofsheep.co.uk/2020/06/04/a-brown-new-deal

Books by Tim Watkins

The Consciousness of Sheep

The Consciousness of Sheep provides a detailed and thoroughly researched explanation of the current predicament of Western civilisation; the ways in which the crises are likely to unfold; and the progressive responses that are beginning to emerge. It is a fascinating read for anyone interested in energy, economics, the environment, and the future of the human race. The message is stark but ultimately positive – it is time for us to develop a sustainable way of life for all of humanity.

Why Don't Lions Chase Mice?

In Why Don't Lions Chase Mice, Tim Watkins explains that without a theory of energy and with a poor and erroneous theory of money, the "experts" and politicians charged with leading us out of the gathering crises – banking and financial collapse, unemployment, under-employment and depression, energy shortages, resource depletion, environmental destruction and climate change – are leading us down a blind alley. Only when we understand the essential role of energy in the economy can we properly understand the stark choices before us.

Decline and Fall: the Brexit years

On 23 June 2016 the British political landscape changed forever. Against the advice of the establishment, the British people had unexpectedly voted to leave the European Union; something that none of the political leaders had planned for. In *Decline and Fall: the Brexit years*, Tim Watkins sets out the long process of decline which provides the context in which the three years of political tragicomedy that followed the result should properly be seen; before presenting a compilation of three-years' of Brexit-related articles from his *Consciousness of Sheep* website.

The Root of all Evil: The problem of debt-based money:

When the Mafia make money they use the same plates, paper and ink as the government. They include the same security features and use the same serial numbers. Even to the most trained eyes this counterfeit currency is physically indistinguishable from the real thing. This being the case, why – exactly – is this Mafia money a crime? Who are its victims? Why should we care? The answers to these questions draw us into the fraud at the heart of our contemporary financial system; a fraud so vast in its scope yet so cleverly disguised that almost all of us treat it as normal while less than one in a million ever sees it. It is the fraud of debt-based money.

The Energy Theory of Value... and its consequences:

Karl Marx was 95 percent correct when he reasoned that one or more of the inputs into production must be paid far less than the value it generates in order to produce profit or "surplus value" at the end. Marx arrived at the blindingly obvious – and entirely wrong – conclusion that this input was labour. What Marx began to see toward the end of his life was that while labour could be exploited, automation meant that something else must be generating surplus value... That "something else" turns out to be *Energy!*

Britain's Coming Energy Crisis:

We dare not talk about this... Politicians dare not discuss it for fear of causing mass panic... North Sea oil and gas production peaked in 1999. The oil bonanza is over – the oil income spent. Britain is once again an energy importer. Worse still, we are increasingly dependent upon imports from the world's trouble spots and hostile regimes – Libya, Nigeria, several Gulf States and Russia. Even worse, successive governments have failed to invest in new electricity generation; let alone a switch from petroleum-powered vehicles…

Austerity… will kill the economy

The same message has been trotted out time and again by economists and politicians from all parties: "We must pay off the debt," "We have to balance the books," "We should have fixed the roof when the sun was shining," "Only by cutting public spending can we hope to return to economic growth." What if they are wrong? What if austerity causes recession? The early cuts triggered a recession, and economic growth has been anaemic ever since. What if these are the direct consequence of a misguided policy of austerity?

ON MENTAL HEALTH

DEFEAT DEPRESSION: A SELF-HELP GUIDE

Defeat Depression is the latest self-help book from Tim Watkins. It builds upon his earlier Depression Workbook and incorporates information on the new science of willpower. This explains why so many of us fall back into habits of thought and behaviour that exacerbate depression; and what we can do to overcome them. The book offers the reader a comprehensive approach to self-help for depression that actually works.

Defeat Depression is written in plain language, and provides the reader with 80 self-help techniques that can be easily included in a daily routine in order to begin the journey out of depression. The publication of Defeat Depression is timely, as its author, Tim Watkins explains:

"Depression has always been with us. But since the economic downturn in 2008, more and more people have developed the condition. Sadly, the consequence of this is that therapies like CBT (cognitive behavioural therapy) and mindfulness have become even harder to access. Far too many people are being left with little more than a packet of pills and a sicknote.

"However, many people affected by depression – myself included – have struggled to understand what helps and what hinders recovery. Drawing on both my own experience and my research among many others affected by depression, I have developed a structure that allows individuals with depression to understand the self-help process and to develop simple lifestyle changes that promote recovery."

As Watkins explains in Defeat Depression, self-help is neither an alternative nor a complement to conventional treatments like antidepressants and talking therapies. Rather, conventional treatments are an important part of a much broader process of self-help in which we learn to promote our own mental wellbeing and manage our own recovery from common mental illnesses like anxiety and depression.

No More Panic

Half of us will experience a panic attack at some time in our lives. For those who do, the experience can be quite literally terrifying. For many the experience is so unpleasant that they avoid similar situations in future. Some develop disabling panic disorders and agoraphobia.

At several times in his life - especially during a severe episode of mixed anxiety and depression, author Tim Watkins experienced disabling panic attacks. Then, quite by accident, he discovered a secret about panic attacks that led to recovery and to his never having a panic attack again.

In this book, he sets out what he - and others - have learned about panic attacks, and how anyone can overcome them... Permanently.

HELPING HANDS: HOW TO HELP SOMEONE ELSE COPE WITH MENTAL HEALTH PROBLEMS

Did you know that the worst thing people do when a family member, friend, neighbour or colleague is struggling with mental health problems, **is to do nothing?** Not out of spite or stigma, but ironically, because most of us are scared of saying or doing the wrong thing.

This is why I wrote Helping hands. Helping Hands helps to make you a skilled lay-helper, providing appropriate support and encouragement to the person you care about.

Helping Hands will provide you with an understanding of wellbeing, and knowledge of mental illness, and will show you how you can help and support someone who has, or is at risk of developing, a mental health problem.

Helping Hands also sets out a great deal of what has been learned about self-help and self-management strategies for recovery from mental illness over the last 25 years.

Printed in Great Britain
by Amazon